NII
LAMPTEY

THE
CURSE
OF PELÉ
NII
LAMPTEY

JORIS KAPER

First published by Pitch Publishing, 2023

Pitch Publishing
9 Donnington Park,
85 Birdham Road,
Chichester,
West Sussex,
PO20 7AJ
www.pitchpublishing.co.uk
info@pitchpublishing.co.uk

© 2023, Joris Kaper
Translation by: Translation Kings

A CIP catalogue record is available for this book
from the British Library.

ISBN 978 1 80150 131 6

Typesetting and origination by Pitch Publishing

Printed and bound in Great Britain by TJ Books Limited, Padstow, Cornwall

Contents

Foreword by Michel Verschueren

SOMEWHERE IN the summer of 1989, Jean Dockx spoke to me. Jean was assistant coach at Anderlecht at the time and he had just returned from Scotland. He was there together with scout Roland van Ginderachter at the World Cup for players under the age of 16. Jean was very enthusiastic about a player they had seen shine there. His name was Nii Lamptey, a 14-year-old from Ghana. Apparently he was someone with a lot of potential. Roland and Jean were lyrical about him and wanted to bring him to Anderlecht. They were in a hurry because several clubs were after him. I liked the idea. I agreed to bring him to Belgium.

The story about how Nii entered Belgium is now known. That didn't go quite right. We enlisted our player Stephen Keshi to convince Lamptey to come to Anderlecht, not knowing how he would do it. The surprise was great when Stephen called me early one morning in August 1989. He was standing at Zaventem airport, together with Nii. I then hopped in my car to pick them up there. When he arrived at the airport, Nii was found to be in possession of a false passport. We still had to arrange that in the right way in Belgium, but luckily we succeeded. As a result, Nii was still able to play football at Anderlecht.

At Anderlecht, Nii was immediately in the spotlight and there was a lot of media interest because he was a talented guy. The way in which he came to Belgium wasn't an issue at the time. Later, when that story became known, there was a lot to do. Anderlecht and I were accused quite a lot with that case. But I can safely say that we acted fairly. In any case, we were happy that Nii was with us, because he could play football. He quickly went into the first team with Anderlecht, led by Aad de Mos. De Mos believed in Nii. His debut was fine, and he did very well in his first season.

Unfortunately things slowly went a bit wrong after that. In the seasons that followed Nii gradually broke away from the club. I don't know if that was because of his agent. I don't really want to say too much about that, but he did completely mislead Nii and made him promises that he didn't keep. That went wrong, and that's a shame. Due to the influence of others, Nii became untenable for us, and he left the club.

Aad de Mos was now trainer at PSV and then also took Nii to Eindhoven. He was then transferred to Aston Villa, and later played football in all kinds of different places around the world. Nii was known as a great talent when he joined Anderlecht. But he was ultimately unable to live up to the high expectations, it's that simple. But that was partly due to personal issues and all kinds of outside influences. All of this influenced his career as a footballer.

Nii has been through a lot during his life and football career. We'd sometimes hear those stories. We didn't hear about certain things until years later. You wouldn't wish such events on anyone.

Yaw Preko, also a former Anderlecht footballer and also from Ghana, was here a few years ago. I then heard from him how Nii was doing, that he lives in Ghana and has founded a school and a football academy there. He trains and guides talented football players there, and he tries to be a help. It satisfies me to hear this.

Nii was a very sweet boy, really. I cannot say a bad word about him. Nii has faced all kinds of problems in his career, as well as in his private life. But he has overcome everything. It makes me happy to hear that he has put all the misery behind him and is now happy at last.

Michel Verschueren, Anderlecht

Foreword by Aad de Mos

THE ANDERLECHT people were impressed by Nii Lamptey when he joined the club. I'd just started as a coach there a few months earlier and I too was impressed. Nii started in the youth team at the Neerpede training complex, but not for long. I went there every now and then and Lamptey was great. I quickly let him train with the first team. Not much later, Yaw Preko and Isaac Asare also came from Ghana to Brussels. Nii was on the bench for the first time during a European Cup match against Dortmund and made his debut a few days later. Everyone was waiting for that. His debut was fine, he even scored. In the matches that followed he gradually started to play in the starting line-up. In every game he showed himself skilled and regularly scored goals. He made himself heard immediately.

In the second season, things went a bit in the wrong direction. Nii ended up in the hands of Antonio Caliendo, an Italian agent. On the one hand he meant well for him, or at least that was the impression I got. Caliendo was the biggest player agent in Europe at the time, and he quite liked Nii. He allowed Nii to choose a new car, and also gave him an expensive watch with his name engraved on it. While he wasn't really that well-known yet, Nii was enamoured by that sort of thing. He also started to behave differently. He sometimes ran at the back in fitness training, although he was in no bad shape at all. Yaw Preko, for example, walked all the way at the front. Of the three Ghanaians who were under contract with Anderlecht, Nii was the star. Preko and Asare hadn't built up their names at the time. Nii could make the difference, although he sometimes slipped a bit defensively. That was a disadvantage in those early days at Anderlecht.

In the summer of 1992 Anderlecht and myself parted ways. Then things also went wrong with Nii, because from that moment on he was no longer playing a lot at Anderlecht. The reason remained unclear to me, although injuries also had something to do with it in retrospect. But I knew what he could do and I brought him to PSV the following season, where I had become manager. That's where the click with Nii really started. At PSV he flourished again, even became the club's top scorer together with Arthur Numan. Nii later expressed his gratitude. That season at PSV was important for Nii because he knew that something had to happen after his last season with Anderlecht. I saw a very different kind of player at PSV.

Nii was also well-liked, both by the supporters and players. He was a good boy and had also learned from that last year at Anderlecht in which he hardly played. But in the end he had to return to Anderlecht after that season at PSV. He then left for England, and after that I lost track of his career. Nii actually came to a standstill there in football technical terms. It wasn't a good decision. I'm convinced that Antonio Caliendo had an impact on him. The fact that Nii left for the Premier League probably had nothing to do with whether that competition suited him. Rather, it likely had to do with a lot of money.

In the years that followed, I occasionally heard, mostly through journalist friends, where Lamptey was hanging out. That he was in Argentina, or in China. But nobody could tell me why he played football in those countries. Later his name was linked a few times to the clubs where I was manager, such as Vitesse and KV Mechelen. Those were rumours in the media because Lamptey was then in the middle of his world trip. I never saw him play again so I couldn't judge his abilities at the time, let alone bring him to a club.

Nii has been grateful to me for our cooperation at Anderlecht and PSV. He didn't show that at the time. Nii wasn't a big talker, but in later years he said a lot in interviews in newspapers, or on video. Years ago, I saw a video in which journalist Willem Vissers visited Nii in Ghana, at his school. Nii thanked me in the video and said he hadn't forgotten about me. I thought that was very nice of him. And more importantly it was nice to see that he was doing well in Ghana. I thought that was the most important thing. Because the stories I had been told over the years were not exactly cheering me up.

Aad de Mos, Anderlecht manager 1989–1992

Chapter 1

Sleeping in the streets

WHEN I think back to when I was a little boy, I see a happy and cheerful child playing football in the street. I don't remember much from the past, but I can distinctly recall that mental image. It's dear to me, it's the oldest memory I have. I often think back to that time. It was so carefree. I played football with whatever I could find on the street. Oranges from market stalls were a favourite. There were also those little footballs, which were played with a lot because they were cheaper than the game-sized balls.

I could always be found on the street; I was always playing football. Maybe I liked it a little too much. I certainly didn't let school stop me from playing football. I spent more time outside playing soccer than sitting in the classroom at my school, the Roman Catholic School in the Nima neighbourhood of Accra. There was some kind of compulsory education in Ghana but nobody enforced it.

The school teachers didn't care. If I was absent from school, my mother would not be told. She never found out that I hardly ever went. My mother didn't always have money to pay the school fees, but I didn't mind that much. I almost didn't go anyway because I was always outside playing football, even though my mother often told me that it was important to go to school.

So I was mostly outside. You could find me wherever a ball was being kicked. I did make sure to stay a distance away from my home and school most of the time. I didn't want anyone to recognise me and tell my mom I was playing truant. So I usually first went for a walk to other neighbourhoods to play football. As a little boy I would sometimes walk a few kilometres to play football somewhere, and after playing I would walk a few kilometres back home. In between I sometimes stopped at friends' houses and was given some mangos or oranges to eat.

I lived with my mother and my two brothers Odartie and Odarquaye in a family house in Accra, where three of my mother's sisters also lived with their children. Their men all worked and lived in a different city. We were with seven children in total, and I also had four nephews. My grandmother also lived in our house until she passed away one day. My grandfather lived in another city because of his work. Such a family home is a normal phenomenon in Ghana. My mother worked at AMA, the Accra Metropolitan Assembly, in the department responsible for keeping the city and the environment clean. With her job she had to take care of three children on her own. My father didn't live with us either; he lived in Kumasi. My parents divorced when I was very young.

I was born in Accra in December 1974. My brothers are a few years younger than me, but I can't remember the time my father lived with us in Accra. I don't know why my parents divorced. I also have no idea how my parents met; I never asked. So I grew up in Accra without a father. I sometimes thought about him but I can't say that I missed his presence. I didn't care that he didn't live with us, I took it for what it was. I wasn't too concerned about that sort of thing. All I cared about was football.

After all the games on the street, I often didn't feel like going home. I wasn't afraid that my mother would find out that I sometimes didn't go to school; it was for a different reason. While I was playing football outside, my brothers and cousins helped with the housework. We weren't all that far apart in age. However, my aunts also expected me to help at home. They were not happy that I often came home just to eat and did not help. Sometimes I didn't get anything to eat because I hadn't done anything to serve the household. Later on, my aunts started beating me too. My aunts sometimes beat me with a cane, and sometimes I had to fetch water as punishment. We did have water pipes at home but that was just meant as a punishment. Then I had to walk somewhere with a big barrel, fill it with water and then walk back home with it. It was a long walk, and very hard for a little boy like me. I became afraid of being punished because of that, and I didn't dare to go home anymore. I would much rather sleep on the street. I slept under buses, in an abandoned kiosk or under a market stall. Not really a safe thing to do as a child. Of course it comes with risks, but I didn't have much of a choice. And as a child you don't think much about possible dangers.

In my memory, the danger wasn't really so bad. If I had to do the same thing now I'd think twice, because I now know the dangers. But I didn't at the time, and because of my home situation this was still the better option. I often slept in my own neighbourhood, sometimes even close to my house. That kept it somewhat familiar. My mother was afraid to say anything about it to her older sisters. That's how it often works in Ghana: people are expected to listen to and respect older people. She therefore kept her mouth shut. My mother was worried I wouldn't come home but she reassured herself that at least I wasn't being beaten by my aunts. And she also suspected that I often slept near our house in the neighbourhood. Only when my aunts left for work in the morning did I dare to go back inside.

Unlike me, my brothers didn't play football very often. Odartie still tried. I took him to a few games to compete but he wasn't much of a runner. That was not successful! He also liked boxing and wanted to become a boxer but in his first fight he got completely beat up in the ring. From that moment on he concentrated on his schoolwork.

When I was about nine years old I signed up for Great Farcos, one of the many youth teams in Accra. That seemed like something good for me, and a boy I knew introduced me to the club. It was the first club I played at, a colts club, a well-known phenomenon in Ghana. They are youth teams put together by mostly well-to-do men. Those teams then play against other colts clubs. They are often composed of boys from certain neighbourhoods and communities. Schools also participate in that system and then play against each other. It doesn't matter where; separate accommodation and competitions don't exist, at least they didn't when I was little. You just play against each other somewhere in the city, on a playing field, a piece of undeveloped land or in a schoolyard. It was and is seen as the backbone of football in Ghana.

Sometimes I played four games a day. Usually, they were 30-minute, seven-against-seven matches. When we were done with a game we then walked to another neighbourhood to play again there. That was the only thing that interested me, playing football as much as possible. Sometimes it also happened that I slept near the place where I played my last game that day. I didn't want to sleep at home anyway, but I also didn't feel like walking back to my own neighbourhood. Those moments were especially difficult because then you were sleeping on the street in a strange neighbourhood and that just felt different from in your own neighbourhood.

I didn't always get to play much at Great Farcos. Most of the players were much bigger than me, and I was very small. I couldn't compete with them and that's why I didn't always play as much. I looked for another team and then wanted to switch to Mohammedans, another colts club in Accra. Because all teams and players had to register at a registration office, I went there together with someone from Mohammedans to sign. But there happened to be someone from Great Farcos at the station as well. He knew why we were there and didn't want me to sign with Mohammedans at all. He tried to prevent that transfer. He yelled that I belonged to Great Farcos and was not allowed to sign with Mohammedans. He kept getting angrier to the point that both men started fighting! In the end the police had to step in to separate them. One police officer then also took me back home. When my mom saw me coming with that cop, she was scared and started crying. She thought I had done something I shouldn't have done, because I would just hang out on the street a lot. But the officer explained what had happened, that two grown men had fought over my transfer. My mother couldn't handle things like that. She thought I would become a nuisance and that was one of the reasons she decided that I should go and live with my father in Kumasi. At the same time she also tried to protect me by deciding that, because that way I would no longer be mistreated by my aunts.

When I heard that, I was especially sad. I was 10 or 11 years old and I would have to miss my mother and brothers. At the same time I also knew that I was not doing well at home. Children should not be abused and sleep on the street, so I was also relieved when I left for Kumasi. But it was strange going to my father. I didn't know him at all; I had never had contact with him in Accra, not even by telephone. So I had no memories of him either. But still I had to live with him. The only things I knew about my father I had heard from my grandfather, who sometimes spoke to me about him.

That's how I knew my father worked in a garage where he was a car mechanic.

In Accra I didn't play football for a long time at a club, at the most two years. I didn't spend a long time at Great Farcos because I didn't get to play much and therefore wanted to go to another team. I was eventually registered with Mohammedans, but I never played a match for them because pretty soon after that transfer I had to go to my father in Kumasi.

My father had remarried to another woman, and with her he had three sons: Papanii, George and Niiquaye Lamptey, my half-brothers. I didn't really bond with them when I lived there because they were much younger than me. But the relationship with my stepmother especially wasn't good right from the start and my initial period in Kumasi was tough. She had a lot of influence on my father, and she quickly let me know that I was not wanted in their house at all. Everything I did was wrong in her eyes. I always wanted to play football, but she didn't like that. She also thought that I should do chores at home and help with the household. She was always very aggressive towards me. And, unfortunately, my father often went along with that. When he came home from work my stepmother told him what I had done wrong.

My father also abused me at times like that. When he was really angry, he would sometimes hit me with his belt or his cane. At one point I couldn't even cry anymore. Apparently I had been beaten so many times that I seemed to be used to it. And because hitting apparently didn't always work anymore, my father decided that he should try new forms of punishment. Those became burning cigarette butts, which he pressed out on me. I still have a few scars from this on my stomach and back. Whether alcohol also contributed to his violent behaviour, I do not know. You don't realise that when you're young. My father was a heavy drinker. Sometimes he made me buy booze because he didn't want other people to see him do it. I had to do that very carefully so that no one noticed what I was doing. Sometimes we would have little food at home. I would get something to eat, but then there would hardly be anything left for him. He would have bought alcohol with the rest of the money he had. He gave me the food and he only drank before going to sleep. He would rather drink than eat. The fact that he also smoked made it even more unhealthy for him.

One of the first things I did when I moved to live in Kumasi was find a new club. In the neighbourhood where my father lived, Aboabo, were Kaloum Stars. Shortly after arriving in Kumasi I went to the Stars to sign up. I was allowed to play a few times so they could test me, but I was soon told I could stay. It was the first time that I actually received training. At the colts clubs in Accra we only held matches.

In Kumasi I ended up at the Sepe Tinpom School. I remember the name, but I don't even know how to spell it correctly. But in Kumasi I didn't take school seriously either. I only went once in a while. Then when I was at school, I sometimes got strange looks because they weren't used to my attendance. A teacher would say to me, 'Hey Nii, what are you doing here at school?' At first they were angry, but at some point they just accepted it. What else were they supposed to do?

My thoughts were only on football, nothing else. The only other thing I can remember is that I did some athletics in school. I was very fast. I used to occasionally go to school for that. I also played table tennis at school, but that was about it. Boxing is very popular in Ghana but it was not for me. So I could be found at school for sports tournaments because I was very good at competing. I felt good about that and I was proud. I was even selected for a regional school football team to represent Kumasi at a national tournament. So even though I was hardly ever at school, I was chosen for those kinds of events. I remember one such tournament.

My school was supposed to play a football tournament but I wasn't allowed to participate because my father hadn't paid the school fees. However, some girls thought that I should take part anyway because I could play football well. They then all collected money to pay my school fees so that I could still participate. I was about 12 years old then.

At the end of my primary school period I had to take exams. We had an exam week that included English, mathematics and physics. I had to register for these but again my father had not paid the fees, so I wasn't allowed to take them. I don't know why the fees were not paid by my father because he wanted me to go to school, he said that often enough. It must have had something to do with money. But it didn't bother me either, because even if he paid I barely went. When I got home the first day of that exam week I lied to my father that I had taken the exams and that they had gone well. But I hadn't even been to school. The second day it went like this again, until the end of the exam week. I never took those exams and of course I didn't get a diploma.

In the meantime, due to my bad home situation, I became more and more rebellious. The more my dad said school was important the more I stayed away. And if he thought I shouldn't hang out with someone, I did. There came a point when my stepmother was fed up. She told my father that he had to choose between her and me. She threatened to pack her things and leave if he chose me. He took her side, which meant I had to leave the house. I was no longer wanted and it was painful. My father thought I should go back to my mother in Accra. But I didn't like that idea. Going back to my aunts who abused me was not an option for me.

At Kaloum Stars I explained the situation, that my stepmother didn't want me in the house anymore so that I had to go back to Accra but didn't want to. I asked if they could do something for me. Alhaji Salifu Abubakar, the chairman, then decided to talk to my father. He was willing to offer me shelter and came to an agreement with my father. He didn't think that was a problem and I would live at home with Salifu. Although it was not nice to hear that I had to leave my father's house, I wasn't very sad. I loved football so much and at Salifu's I could play without fear of being mistreated. That was a nice prospect. Salifu's house was located in the compound of Kaloum Stars. I even slept in the same room as Salifu. Sometimes a few other people stayed on the grounds of the club, but often I was alone with Salifu. Not many other guys slept there. In the end I lasted about half a year, at the most a year, at my father and stepmother's place.

At Kaloum Stars there was one thing that was very different from what I was used to. It was an Islamic football club and they prayed five times a day. In those moments I would just kind of sit by myself. I was not a Muslim; I was raised Catholic. After a while Salifu came to me. He asked me if I wanted to become a Muslim. I decided to go along with that. After all, Salifu and his club had taken me under his wing. It wasn't a hard requirement anyway. If I had remained Catholic I think they would have accepted that too, but I thought it would be the best choice at the time. I really wanted to stay with Kaloum Stars because I didn't really have any other good options for where I could live, so at that time I did everything I could to achieve that goal, and maybe my chances would be better if I became a Muslim. So I would go through life as a Muslim for the next few years. Once I left my father's house, I didn't speak to him for six months. I didn't even stop by even though we lived in the same neighbourhood.

But one day I met him. I played a game with Kaloum Stars, where I was dribbling the ball quite a bit. As a result I was hit hard by an opponent a few times. Suddenly I heard someone whistling in a certain way. It was exactly the way my father always whistled when he called me. I was distracted for a moment and thought it was a coincidence.

But then I heard it again. I looked in the direction of where the whistling was coming from. Then I saw my father standing there. He motioned for me to come to him. He knelt and then said something I will never forget. He said, 'Nii, if you want to play football for a long time, you shouldn't dribble the ball so much.' I went back on to the field, heeded my father's advice, and scored twice. My father then went back home. I was very surprised that he came to watch. I even thought it was very funny.

The next day I visited him and spoke to him for the first time in half a year. Online I've read a lot of nonsense about my father and the period I lived in Kumasi; that he would argue with people from Kaloum Stars, that he would come over in a drunken stupor to berate me. That is not true. He didn't go there to argue. It was advice, good advice even, that my father gave me at that game. What is true is that he was not happy with the fact that I had become a Muslim. Once when I was praying in a mosque, I had just gotten on my knees to pray. Suddenly my father entered the mosque, hit me hard on the butt and then ran out again. I just went on praying but I was very surprised. Now I can laugh about it, but then I was really dumbfounded.

In the period that I lived with Salifu everything went pretty well. I could finally play football without fear of being abused at home. At Kaloum Stars, however, I could only continue playing football until I was about 13 years old. After that I would have to make the switch to a youth team at a big club.

Most clubs had a second team, usually for boys up to the age of 17. I was happy for the moment at having to leave. I didn't really realise that I was better than my peers, but it was apparently quite well known among the people who were involved in football. During a Kaloum Stars game, a player from Cornerstones, a club from Kumasi that was playing in the Ghanaian Premier League at the time, was present. He was apparently impressed because he informed the management of the Stars and asked me if I wanted to go for a few trial training sessions with his club, which of course I wanted to. He picked me up a few days later on his bike for training at Cornerstones. The management were satisfied because after a few sessions they had seen enough. They promised me a lot of playing time, which made me decide to go to Cornerstones. At that time I was also able to go to Asante Kotoko, the most popular club in Ghana. Salifu was disappointed that I didn't choose Kotoko because he was a big fan of that club. But I wouldn't get around to playing there as much as I would at Cornerstones, so it wasn't a difficult choice for me.

With the Cornerstones youth team we often had to play football before the first-team games. So, before they played, it was our turn first. At one point I had to play for Cornerstones in Accra. It had been two and a half or three years since I had left for Kumasi. We played against Great Olympics in Accra and I was about 13 years old. I don't remember much about the game itself, but it was very important to me. After that match, a nephew of mine suddenly walked up to me. He had seen me playing. I was very surprised. I still have no idea how he knew I was playing football there and that I had signed with Cornerstones. There had been no contact. In fact, since I left for Kumasi I had no contact with my family in Accra, including my mother and brothers. Perhaps it was pure coincidence that he saw me there, of course that was possible, and he was there because he wanted to see the game between Cornerstones and Great Olympics.

I immediately asked my nephew how my mother was doing. He said she had already left the family home. She had remarried and now lived elsewhere in Accra. I asked the club for permission to stay an extra day in Accra so that I could visit my mother. That was allowed, luckily. I visited her and saw her for the first time in two and a half, maybe three years. Of course it was very nice to see her and my brothers again after such a long time. In the meantime, my mother had married Jim Armahtey, a radio host at GBC, Ghana's first TV and radio station. So he became my stepfather, although I didn't regard him in that way. After all, he never took care of me, and we never lived together. I only met him for the first time when he was already married to my mother. But I got on quite well with him as he wasn't like my stepmother. Unfortunately I could only stay with my mother for one day. But since then we tried keeping in touch again even though that was very difficult in Ghana. Even making a phone call was sometimes difficult, and cell phones and the internet didn't exist yet. My mother and Jim would later have two more sons, Armahken and Armah, and one daughter, Ahene, my half-brothers and half-sister.

While that meeting with my family was very nice, that's not the biggest reason why that match was very important in retrospect. As a result of the game I received an invitation for the Ghana under-16 national team. Afterwards, someone from the Ghana Football Association entered the locker room and told the coach that someone from his team had been selected for Ghana under-16s. That was me. It was a dream come true. A national youth team! The following week I had to report back to Accra for a training camp. That's how my football career really started, though I didn't know that at the time.

Chapter 2

The new Pelé

WHEN I was called up to Ghana under-16s for the first time, it was a great honour. Of course I was very happy, but that was about it. I didn't even think about a career as a professional footballer, let alone making money from the sport. I played football because I liked it, just like almost all the other boys back then. It was purely for fun and nothing more. Today that's almost impossible to imagine. Boys who start playing football nowadays dream of a career abroad and earning a lot of money. We never had those thoughts before. In fact, we didn't even know such a thing was possible.

In the summer of 1989 FIFA hosted the U-16 World Cup and Africa sent three countries after a qualifying tournament. The Ghana national federation had only recently started, in 1986, with an under-16 team called the Black Starlets – a diminution of the national team's nickname, the Black Stars. So everything was still fairly new for us all.

I still remember my first international for Ghana's under-16s. We played against Cameroon in Accra on 2 September 1988 in a qualifying match for the U-16 World Cup. I was only 13 years old and was really still a kid. In the first round we were supposed to play against Togo but they withdrew, a well-known phenomenon in African tournaments at the time. There was simply too little money available, especially for youth teams. So without playing we went through to the second round where Cameroon were the opponents. At home we won 1-0 but two weeks later we lost the away game 2-1, although based on the away goals rule we went through to the next round where we had to play against Ivory Coast, and the winner would go to the World Cup.

In the build-up to those qualifiers we went on a training camp to Brazil. It was the first time being outside Africa for most of the boys, so everyone was delighted and there was a very excited atmosphere. I don't know why we went to Brazil specifically, but I just went with it. Maybe it was to do with the facilities. We ended up staying there for about six weeks. Just before we were about to go back someone suggested that we could do some shopping. We'd all made some money and some of the guys wanted to buy something nice with it. For example, Yaw Preko, one of my team-mates, bought a radio. A couple of guys got colour TVs. You should know now that the voltage in Ghana is 240v, but most of the guys didn't understand that. In Brazil they had a different voltage, so they all bought TVs built for different power.

After we got back to Ghana we also had to spend a week or two in a training camp there. In the rooms the boys immediately unpacked their televisions to try them out, but they didn't get to see much more than black-and-white images. Little did they know that those TVs didn't work well in Ghana! Everyone walked into the room together to see if that was the case with every television, and it turned out to be so. We never went to another continent so we didn't know about other voltages and things like that. They took the TVs apart, checked if the wires and all parts were properly connected. Nothing helped. The boys who hadn't bought a TV were doubled over with laughter and they joked about that for a long time. Fortunately for them, a repairman eventually came by and said it was the voltage. He then provided adapters that solved the problem.

On 8 January 1989 we played the first of our two decisive qualifiers, an away game at the Ivory Coast. We held on by drawing 1-1. Two weeks later we won 2-0 and with that we qualified for the World Cup. Nigeria and Guinea had also qualified on behalf of Africa.

It was the first time that the Black Starlets had qualified for the U-16 World Cup. This made sense because the team hadn't existed for very long. But it was also the first time that a representative team of Ghana qualified for a World Cup final stages. In Ghana there was a lot of attention given to that achievement. The World Cup was to be held in Scotland that summer, but none of us knew anything about that country. So we thought it was exciting, and we didn't know what to expect.

I still remember a lot from the World Cup in Scotland in June 1989, especially the happiness in the team. No one had ever been to Europe. Everyone was really looking forward to it and we were all very excited. At the tournament we were divided into a group with Cuba, Bahrain and Scotland. I remember playing against Scotland, of course. We had to face them in the opening game at the large Hampden Park in Glasgow. That game ended 0-0 but the match stayed with me for a completely different reason. Pelé was present in the stadium and, afterwards, he was the one who had to pick a man of the match. He chose me. The great Pelé chose me! On the field, an Asian man approached me and handed me the accompanying trophy. Pelé himself apparently would not. But my joy was no less, although that wasn't the most important thing. That occasion left me with more than a trophy. After the match Pelé said to the press the infamous words that would haunt me for the rest of my career. He had seen the new Pelé, his natural successor.

That was me. Nii Lamptey was the new Pelé. Nice words, although I didn't realise their impact at the time.

The statement made headlines the next day. It was also discussed in Ghana, and also in the team. I didn't really know how to respond. I liked hearing it but to be honest I hardly knew anything about Pelé at the time. I'd heard his name before, but that was it. Can you imagine that? I didn't read, so I wouldn't see newspapers or magazines that he could be in. I didn't watch TV either and the internet didn't exist yet. I was always outside playing football. How was I supposed to know who Pelé was? So I didn't dwell too much on his words at that time. I was mainly busy with the next matches, because we still had two to play in the group.

But because everyone was talking about that statement, in the days and weeks that followed I started to investigate a little bit about who Pelé was. I asked for information from acquaintances and later I went to watch videotapes of him. The impact of his infamous words was therefore not so great on me at the moment he uttered them. But the more

I learned about him afterwards, the more impact they had. That realisation slowly came in the weeks that followed. Only then did I see that it was a great honour to be seen by Pelé as his successor.

Besides his nice words about me, the media were also very positive about our team. But despite that we didn't win in our other two group matches. We lost 1-0 to Bahrain and drew 2-2 against Cuba. After three games the World Cup was over for us. But despite that early elimination our youth team had made an impression, not only at the tournament itself but also in Ghana. We were proud, also because it was the first time for a Ghanaian team at a World Cup.

The atmosphere during and after the World Cup was the same as before the tournament. I wasn't thinking about my future at all; I just wanted to play football. No one in the team was aware that there were opportunities to make money in Europe with football. We were so young and naive. We played for fun, and that remained the same after the tournament.

We didn't know that these kinds of tournaments had a great appeal for scouts from European clubs. Today it is different, but for us everything was new. After that World Cup people suddenly came to me and expressed their interest. I really didn't care about that before. What do you expect? I was just a kid; I was only 14. I knew nothing about that. Apparently I hadn't just impressed Pelé at that tournament. A few clubs showed interest: Glasgow Rangers, Queens Park Rangers, Vasco da Gama, and Anderlecht. Scouts from those clubs were present at that tournament but I didn't talk to anyone else, I just went back to Ghana with the team.

* * *

On behalf of the Belgian club Anderlecht, assistant coach Jean Dockx and scout Roland van Ginderachter were present at the U-16 World Cup. Van Ginderachter was a modest football player at, among others, RFC Tournai, and Racing White Brussels. Dockx had been a player with Anderlecht, where he had celebrated great successes in the 1970s, winning the European Cup Winners' Cup twice, the European Super Cup, the Belgian Cup four times and the Belgian title twice. After he finished playing, Dockx started a coaching career, which brought him back to Anderlecht in 1984, this time as an assistant coach.

In Scotland, Dockx and Van Ginderachter watched Roberto Carlos from Brazil and Luís Figo from Portugal: two players who would later become world champions. In the years that followed, Figo wore the shirts of Barcelona, Real Madrid and Inter Milan. With those clubs he would win eight national titles, the European Cup Winners' Cup, the Champions League and a World Cup. Roberto Carlos would win the Spanish title four times, the Champions League three times and the Intercontinental Cup twice with Real Madrid, and the 2002 World Cup with Brazil. However, Dockx had his eye on someone else: 14-year-old Nii Lamptey from Ghana.

Van Ginderachter was also enthusiastic. Their report ended up on the desk of 'Mister' Michel Verschueren, who has been acting as manager at Anderlecht since 1980. On the intercession of chairman Constant Vanden Stock he was snatched from RWDM and brought to Anderlecht. In the years that followed Verschueren was, among other things, the driving force behind the renovation of the club's stadium.

Verschueren: 'At that time I had known Jean for years and had very good contact with him. Jean was a very sweet man. Always civilised, friendly and correct. And he always stayed in his role as an assistant coach, but also as a scout. He never tried to jump over anyone else's head. And he was a real football connoisseur. He had a good vision of modern football. Unfortunately, Jean passed away unexpectedly in 2002 from a heart attack. He left much too early.

'Jean had been present at that youth World Cup and had submitted a report about one Nii Lamptey to the youth committee of Anderlecht. After all, the boy was only 14 years old. I got to see that report through Philippe Collin, who was the youth chairman at the time. Collin was a cousin of Roger Vanden Stock, who in turn was the son of Anderlecht chairman Constant Vanden Stock. The gist of Jean's report was quite simple: I had to go straight to Ghana to try and sign Lamptey. And fast. I was fine with it, but I couldn't go that way myself. At the time, the club was not run as it is now. Now more than 100 people work here, not counting the players and technical staff. At the time there were maybe a dozen or so. Therefore I had absolutely no time to go to Ghana myself, I had to run the club. Moreover, Jean had said that it would be a difficult job to get Lamptey to Belgium. Not only because other clubs were interested, but also because his passport was confiscated by the Ghanaian Football Association. They wouldn't cooperate.'

Yaw Preko was Nii's team-mate in the Ghana under-16 squad. Preko, who was also 14 years old, then played for Powerlines in Ghana: 'The Ghanaian Football Association wanted to keep us together after the World Cup in Scotland. We did quite well at that World Cup, even though we didn't survive the group stage. They wanted to prepare us well for the next youth World Cup, in 1991. That is why our passports were confiscated. Then they could keep the team together. They didn't want the team to fall apart because players would leave.'

Nii: 'It wasn't just my passport that was confiscated. They had done that to everyone on the team. We all travelled to Scotland together, and it was also intended that we would all return to Ghana again. That was the first time the union did that; it had never happened before. Incidentally, that happened at the behest of the Ghanaian president himself, not so much the football association. Jerry Rawlings was president of Ghana at the time. He directly ordered the football association to confiscate our passports so that the team would stay together. Rawlings was a big football fan. Nowadays you no longer have that kind of government interference, that would be illegal. But at the time, politics could still exert a lot of influence on the football association.'

Verschueren: 'So I didn't have time to travel to Ghana myself. But we were lucky at Anderlecht that Stephen Keshi was under contract with us. Truly an athlete. A heavy, strong guy, he played well at Anderlecht. Keshi was also the captain of the Nigerian national team at the time and one of the greatest players in all of Africa. I then called him to me and asked, "Stephen, could you do something for me?" "Yes of course Mister Michel, what should I do for you?" "Do you know a Nii Lamptey, a football player from Ghana?" He agreed that he knew Nii. "Can you help me get this player to Anderlecht?" "No problem, Mister Michel," he said. A few weeks later, he was selected for the Nigeria national team. He told me he would try to help me get Lamptey to Brussels.'

Preko: 'Keshi was an icon of African football. He needed no introduction in Africa, he was the big man. If you wanted to get something done in African football, you just had to play it through him. And that is exactly what Anderlecht did. Keshi really was like a president in Africa. All he had to do was snap his fingers. So, Verschueren's assignment was perhaps not that difficult for him.'

Keshi's European football career started in 1986 at the Belgian club KSC Lokeren. He had already been active in Nigeria and the Ivory Coast for several years, and also for a few years internationally. With his transfer to Belgium he was one of the first Nigerians to find his way to Europe, paving the way for other African footballers. It gave him prestige on the entire African continent. And while many had never seen him play football, everyone knew his name. Keshi was having a good season at Lokeren and after just one season he signed with Anderlecht, where he would stay until the summer of 1991. Keshi's hero status became definitive when Nigeria won the Africa Cup of Nations under his captaincy in 1994. In the same year, Nigeria also made their first appearance at the World Cup.

In a 2010 documentary by the Belgian sports programme *Belga Sport*, Keshi spoke about Nii's transfer and journey: 'I came to Mister Michel, and he asked me to go to Ghana. Apparently there was a player walking around that everyone was chasing. I had to make sure that he would come to Anderlecht. When I left for Nigeria a few weeks later for international obligations, Verschueren said, "Don't forget!" I replied, "Yes Mister Michel, no problem!"'

* * *

In July 1989, a few weeks after the World Cup in Scotland, we were back in a training camp in Accra. In between two training sessions a man came up to me. He introduced himself as the manager of Stephen Keshi. I had no idea what Keshi looked like, but I knew his name and reputation. Keshi was a big name in Africa. No sooner had the manager introduced himself than he had already given me his card. That was the first thing he did. It said something like 'local agent Nigeria Stephen Keshi'. He told me that Stephen would like to talk to me and that he could accommodate me at a club in Europe. He didn't mention the name of the club, just Keshi's name. I don't remember if he was talking about Belgium, but he wasn't talking about Anderlecht yet. I also only knew Keshi as a Nigerian international. I didn't know he played for Anderlecht in Europe. But I thought: if Keshi wants me to play at his club, why not? I had no plans at all to leave Ghana, but when I heard his name I was immediately sold. The moment when I was told that Keshi wanted to talk to me and that he had a club for me in Europe, it was like a dream come true. I was very happy.

I wanted to go to Keshi in Nigeria to talk, but it was difficult for me to walk away from our training camp at the time. Keshi's agent said Stephen would be back in the Nigerian capital, Lagos, in a few weeks. But before we could talk any longer, the conversation was abruptly ended by some people from the Ghana Football Association. Of course they also knew what Keshi's manager was coming to do. His presence was not appreciated and they became very angry. They were about to attack him and threatened to arrest him. The manager then left quickly. I hadn't even spoken to that man for five minutes, but it was enough to persuade me. I wanted to go to Europe, to Keshi's club.

Chapter 3

The false passport

THE WAY I left Ghana has taken on a life of its own after all these years. I would have been hiding in the back of a car, I would have been taken by people smugglers, I would have pretended to be the son of a taxi driver, I would have been kidnapped or taken on a three-week journey. I've heard and read all variants. Maybe it went that way with other African players, but not with me.

Right after Stephen Keshi's manager came to our training camp, we got two weeks off. That was sometime in the second week of August. Then we had to report back to the training camp. Luckily I had kept Keshi's manager's business card well. It was very smart of him to give that to me right away when he introduced himself. If he had waited a little longer, union people might have seen that and would have taken the card away. It seemed strange at the time, because he gave his card almost before we had said anything to each other. But now I know that was very clever, and I immediately hid the card. It was very important for my career because on it was not only his name, but also his address. Without the card I might never have left.

Since we had time off, I decided it was a good time to visit Keshi's manager. However, there was one big problem: he lived in Lagos, the capital of Nigeria. And I didn't have my passport, it was in the possession of the football association. But I was determined and wanted to go to visit him so I decided to try to travel to Lagos anyway. I felt it would be best if I didn't share my plans with anyone. I didn't even tell my parents what I was up to. My mother was pregnant at the time, and because of the great distance I had little contact with her anyway. And because of the bad relationship with my father, I decided not to tell him anything. Besides, I no longer lived with him, but with Salifu.

In the end I told two people what I was up to. I trusted them. I told Salifu and a former Kaloum Stars team-mate, Osei Kojo. I was already playing for Cornerstones at the time but knew him from Kaloum Stars. Osei was living in Accra when I decided to leave for Nigeria. I was able to spend the night at his home before leaving early the next morning for the bus station. Arriving at the station, I told a minivan bus driver that I had to go to Lagos. But, of course, I didn't have a passport. Fortunately the driver did. In case of trouble along the way he would pretend I was his son. He did, however, charge double the price from $50 to $100. He was doing something he shouldn't so he might also be at risk. And perhaps he could use that money in an emergency to bribe customs officers or agents. Before he agreed, he told me that I would have to get off the bus in advance at every border crossing and cross the border on foot via a detour. He would then be waiting for me a little further away. I agreed to that.

I had almost nothing with me when I left. I walked in flip-flops and, apart from the clothes I was wearing, I only had a plastic bag with me. Inside were some extra clothes and a pair of shoes. Taking more wasn't an option either. To get to Lagos, the bus had to cross three borders – first from Ghana to Togo, then Togo and Benin, and finally Benin and Nigeria. At every border it was the same procedure. Just before we got there I left the bus, after which I crossed via a detour through the undergrowth, and away from customs controls. Once I had crossed the border I walked back to the road, where the van was somewhere waiting for me. I did that at all three crossings. It was terrible and I was very scared, but that's nothing unexpected either. I was only 14 years old. I was alone, my parents didn't know anything about it, and I had to cross a few borders illegally. But I was also determined: I wanted to play football at Keshi's club.

I ran through the undergrowth to get across the border. Fortunately I was very fit. If I got caught then I would be sent back to Ghana, and everything would have been for nothing. Before I crossed the border somewhere, I also met other people along the way. I even passed a police post somewhere. But nobody cared about me. The journey to Lagos took almost a day. I left Accra in the morning and arrived in Lagos early the next day. There I showed Keshi's manager's card to a taxi driver. He drove straight to the address on the card.

Luckily Keshi's manager was home. He was very happy to see me and hugged me. He paid the taxi for me because I didn't have enough money with me, and only then did I hear all the details from him about the club. At that moment it became clear to me that I would go to Anderlecht. They were lucky that Keshi played football there and could get things done in Africa. That's the only reason why I ended up at Anderlecht. Perhaps otherwise I might have ended up somewhere else, because later I heard that other clubs were also interested. Keshi's manager called Stephen to say I was with him. Keshi couldn't believe it. I heard him yell 'no waaaay!' on the phone. He thought it was impossible, firstly because of my confiscated passport, but also because of the way his manager was treated in Accra by the people of the Ghanaian Football Association.

I also briefly talked to Stephen Keshi on the phone. I was happy, a little nervous even. Stephen was, after all, an African football legend. He sounded very happy indeed. 'Nice Nii, so nice to meet you! I'll see you soon!' It was a short conversation but I was glad to hear him. Keshi was also in Lagos at the time with the Nigeria national team. A few days later he would play an international match with Nigeria, so I had to be patient. His manager booked a hotel for me in the meantime, pending Keshi's arrival.

Two days after my arrival in Lagos I met Keshi for the first time. I was exhilarated. I was picked up from my hotel and dropped off at the hotel where Keshi was staying with the national team. There we met for the first time, and he hugged me. After the acquaintance we went to his hotel room, where we could talk quietly. He then also called some people and not much later a few men came by. They greeted me and took a picture of me. At the time I didn't know what that was for. Keshi gave them some money and then told me it was for a new passport. They were back in a few hours with a new passport. I looked at it – it was a Nigerian passport with my photo in it. And I had a new name: Stephen Keshi Junior. I was suddenly Keshi's son! That was very strange, but I just accepted it for what it was. I had no choice. I loved football, I did what I had to do to succeed, so I thought everything was fine even if that meant that I now had a passport that suddenly contained a different name and nationality.

* * *

On 12 August 1989 Stephen Keshi played in a qualifying match for the 1990 World Cup with Nigeria, who were in a group with Cameroon, Gabon and Angola and must win to keep alive their hopes of reaching the finals. Just before half-time against Angola, Keshi scored what turned out to be the only and therefore winning goal.

However, the win was overshadowed by the death of Nigerian player Samuel Okwaraji. While attention was focused on the referee, who had just shown a red card to an Angola player, Okwaraji collapsed on the other side of the field and died of heart failure.

The day after the Nigeria match, we were to leave for Brussels. I was picked up by Keshi's manager at my hotel. At the airport everyone was happy because Nigeria had won the day before. The sad news about Okwaraji didn't seem to get through, at least not that I remember. Keshi was, of course, moved by the news. But it had happened and unfortunately we couldn't change that. He couldn't do anything but accept it and learn to deal with it, no matter how hard that sounds.

Keshi was congratulated or applauded by several people for his goal. At passport control we handed in our passports, and without any hesitation we got a stamp. It was that simple. Nobody made a problem of anything. There was no question at all if I was actually Keshi's son. He was a celebrity in Africa, so no one made things be difficult. And even if they knew I wasn't really Keshi's son, I still wonder if they'd make a fuss about it. Africa at the end of the 1980s was a lot different from how it is now, a lot more could be gotten away with then.

* * *

Verschueren: 'I didn't know how Stephen arranged certain things in Africa. It wasn't until years later that I learned how Nii had ended up in Nigeria from Ghana. I also never spoke to Nii and Stephen when they were in Nigeria. Stephen left for Nigeria for an international match and the next time I spoke to him he was at Brussels Zaventem Airport. That was a few days after his international match. Suddenly I got a phone call at 4am. Surprised, I answered the phone, and it turned out to be Stephen. He said he had a small problem. It was about Nii Lamptey. He asked if I could come to the airport.

'I jumped in my car and hurried to the airport. I was able to get there quite quickly because I live a few kilometres away. That wasn't that hard. I then met Stephen at the airport. He said they were stopped by customs and that Nii was not allowed to enter the country. I asked Keshi about Nii's passport. He gave me the passport. It turned out to be false. "Keshi Jr", it said. Because of that name on the passport, I was very surprised when I saw Nii. That passport made me question whether Stephen really had Nii Lamptey with him. After all, I didn't know what Nii looked like. I had never seen him, not even on videotapes. But I trusted Keshi, so I had to believe it was Nii.'

Nii agrees that that first acquaintance was strange: 'At first Verschueren thought I wasn't really Nii Lamptey, because of that passport. Keshi had to explain it a few times before Verschueren believed it.'

Verschueren: 'Keshi had arranged that false passport in Nigeria on his own initiative. Apparently, that was very easy then. Nii Lamptey, a player of a Ghana youth team, who goes to Anderlecht on a fake Nigerian passport! I said, "Stephen, this is not OK. I'm happy with your help, but this is really not OK." I then took that passport and told him that he had to go back to customs to tell Nii that his passport had been lost. That was the only way to get rid of it. That was accepted there at the time, possibly because we showed that Anderlecht was involved.

'In the meantime, I started arranging the right papers for Nii. I took the fake passport to the Federal Judicial Police in Brussels. I explained the situation there and all the necessary papers for Nii were arranged there. Frans Reyniers helped me with that. He was the head of the Federal Judicial Police in Brussels, but also a supporter of Anderlecht. This certainly contributed to the fact that everything could be arranged very quickly, but he did not do anything in his position that was not allowed. It was a period of relative calm, without terrorism. Things like that could still be arranged easily and quickly. Everything was arranged within a day via Frans.

'As a result, Stephen and Nii had to stay at the airport day and night, until all papers were in order. Without the proper papers, Nii simply could not enter the country. It was of course not possible to enter Belgium under a false name, especially not as a youth international. Apparently those things could be circumvented a little easier in Africa. Likewise with Nii's passport. But in the end I arranged the right papers. I think Nii got temporary papers first, and later his definitive ones. Anyway, from that moment on Nii could legally enter Belgium.'

Nii: 'While Mister Michel was preparing the paperwork, I just had to wait at the airport in Brussels. I just had to kill time. But I was excited, I was happy. I had to wait until the next morning, but it only felt like a few hours. Everything was new there. I was fascinated. All those modern shops over there, I visited them all, just to look around. I just went to explore everything, and I just liked it all. Nosing around in the souvenir shops, eating, drinking coffee, that's how I tried to kill time.'

Verschueren: 'A few years later, Frans Reyniers told the story about Lamptey and only then did it end up in the media. Anderlecht and myself, in particular, were being accused in the media at the time that it was pure human trafficking, kidnapping, that he entered the country as a piece of contraband. But it was dead simple. Lamptey wanted to come to Europe, Anderlecht wanted to recruit him, and Keshi wanted to do me a favour. However, he'd done so in his own way. Nevertheless, Keshi was a great person. Often when he went to Africa, he would take something back for me. A statue or something like that, once even a pair of shoes. I had good contact with him. If there were any problems, he could just come to me, and I would solve it for him.'

Aad de Mos, coach of Anderlecht at the time, was not surprised by the role Keshi played in the transfer from

Lamptey to Anderlecht: 'He already seemed interested in a role as manager or something like that. But he had also been a leader throughout his football career, both on and off the field. He accompanied Nii in Brussels in those early months, and later Isaac Asare and Yaw Preko as well. It wasn't for nothing that his nickname was "Big Boss".'

Nii: 'I hadn't played football for a long time at Cornerstones, not even a year. But because I was still under contract there, Anderlecht contacted them. A delegation from the club then came to Brussels to deal with the youth committee of the club. After all, I was picked up as a youth player. Then everything is completely official. They also realised that there was no point in stopping the transfer. And, of course, they received a transfer fee. That was around $100,000, a decent amount for both clubs. They also took my passport, my real passport, with them from Ghana.'

Yaw Preko remembers well when Nii suddenly stopped showing up for the Ghana youth team: 'We had a few weeks off when Nii left for Nigeria. Our training camps were always long, sometimes a few months. In between we had a few weeks off, but when we came back after those weeks off, Nii was nowhere to be found. He was suddenly gone. You must imagine that it was 1989, there was no internet and even telephone calls were sometimes difficult in Ghana.

So, it was very difficult to find out where he was. Nii had told virtually no one about his plans. We could only guess where he was. We thought he might be in Scotland because we played that World Cup there. Others said he was in England or France.

'In my view Mister Michel had not acted wrong at all. Yes, Nii travelled to Belgium on a false passport, but Verschueren had nothing to do with that. He acted in good faith. And besides, this was a nice step for Nii. Keshi had solved it in a way that is not officially allowed, but to say that it is a crime is going too far for me. It wasn't a big deal in Ghana afterwards either. Nii was destined to go abroad.

'After Nii disappeared, he also stayed away from our youth team for several months without contacting any of us. He stayed away until he signed a contract with Anderlecht, and everything was settled with his old club. I think to make sure he could also return to Belgium. He had of course left with a false passport, and everything had to be arranged with his old club. I can imagine he didn't want to give anyone a reason to keep him in Ghana upon his return. A few months after Nii's disappearance, Jean Pierre Kindermans, a scout from Anderlecht, came to Ghana. We heard from him that Nii was in Belgium, at Anderlecht.

Isaac Asare and I also ended up at Anderlecht through Kindermans in the summer of 1990.'

Nii: 'In Ghana, the big news was that I had suddenly disappeared. They couldn't find me anywhere, and soon there were rumours that I had been kidnapped. I also didn't let my parents know where I was for months. That wasn't very strange, because at that time I hardly spoke to my parents anyway, except for various specific reasons. The relationship I had with them just didn't amount to much at the time. Finally, after about three months I called my mother, who was six months pregnant at the time. She cried with joy when I called her. My father didn't, he reacted completely differently. He was mostly angry. "What are you doing? Where the hell are you?", things like that. In the end, he was affected the worst by the situation, because I was officially living with him. My father didn't know where I was, of course, but the police thought otherwise. They threatened to arrest him because they thought he knew where I was. Eventually my parents understood that I had left for Europe so that I could earn money. I told them both that I would be coming back to Ghana soon, but in the end it took over a year.'

Chapter 4

The first steps in Belgium

WHEN I arrived in Belgium, I was very happy. I can't forget that emotion. You cannot imagine how I felt. I had been to Scotland during the World Cup, which was my first introduction to Europe. I imagined something similar in Belgium. I really liked the city of Brussels from the start. I was young, but luckily Stephen Keshi took me under his wing. He helped me a lot in those early days. He made me forget a lot of things there, and I mean that in a good way – the things from my childhood. It was a new chapter in my life and unlike anything from the years before. Thanks to Stephen and his wife I felt at home quite quickly, although sometimes it was not easy. They took me in when I arrived in Brussels. I felt very privileged to be able to stay with them.

* * *

In the summer that Nii arrived in Belgium, a new trainer had been appointed at Anderlecht: Dutchman Aad de Mos.

The coach had great successes at Ajax and KV Mechelen in the previous years and had earned his move to Anderlecht, who saw in him someone who understood the art of forging a team of both existing stars and new talent.

De Mos: 'I already had a bit of a reputation at the club in that area, especially because of my time at Ajax. There I had worked with many young boys, like Frank Rijkaard, Marco van Basten and John van 't Schip. When I took over from Leo Beenhakker in March 1981, I let Sonny Silooy and Gerald Vanenburg make their debuts, followed in 1983 by John Bosman. Each and every one of those boys became top international players over the years. In 1986 I started at KV Mechelen, but that club, unlike Ajax, did not have a high-quality youth academy. But there I was lucky that chairman John Cordier had big plans for the club. As a result, he made a lot of money available. He wanted to put together a team of talents and veterans.

'I started there in February 1986, after Ernst Künnecke was fired from the club. We managed to maintain ourselves in the highest Belgian league, and in that summer we attracted a few new players, including Michel Preud'homme, Lei Clijsters and Wim Hofkens. The team slowly became a mix of veterans and emerging talents, just as the club envisioned. Partly because of this we finished second in

1986/87, and won the cup for the first time in the club's existence.

'The following season got even better. For me it is the pinnacle of my coaching career. With newcomers such as Pascal De Wilde and Marc Emmers, we were able to compete with Anderlecht. In the end we did not become champions, but as European debutants we did win the European Cup Winners' Cup. That was a resounding stunt, the ultimate football fairytale. We defeated holders Ajax in the final 1-0, thanks to a goal from Piet den Boer. And nobody cared about Mechelen's chances in that final. But Danny Blind already got a red card for Ajax in the 16th minute; that helped of course. But I am convinced that the result would have been the same if that card had not been drawn. And besides, winning that cup was one thing, but beating Ajax in the final made it extra special. My period at Ajax ended abruptly in May 1985, when the group of players made it known to the board that there was too little support for me as a coach. At that time we were first in the league. Without me Ajax became champions only 20 days later.

'The following season we also brought Marc Wilmots and John Bosman to Mechelen and became champions, the club's first league title since 1948. And earlier that season we managed to conquer the European Super Cup at the expense of PSV, the winners of the European Cup. I can imagine that Anderlecht chairman Constant Vanden Stock looked at the successes with sorrow. They were suddenly in the shadow of KV Mechelen. Moreover, Mechelen is only 35 kilometres away from Brussels; it's logical that Vanden Stock suddenly saw the club as a major competitor. His tactics were simple: try to buy the best players in the country and, if necessary, the best coach. Because of the successes with KV Mechelen, he came to me. Before the end of the competition, we agreed a contract for the next season with Anderlecht. And I was also ready for a new challenge. With KV Mechelen I had achieved everything that could be achieved.

'During my Mechelen period, I already started to orientate and put together the Anderlecht selection for the next season. For example, I went to watch Anderlecht under-19 matches. At the start of the new season, I brought three of those guys into the selection: Bertrand Crasson, Philip Osondu and Pär Zetterberg. The selection was also strengthened with Marc Degryse. He was already on my wish list at KV Mechelen, but when I went to Anderlecht he came to Brussels instead of Mechelen. That summer I was talking to the technical staff about the selection, when Jean Dockx told me that he also had someone in mind for the future; one Nii Lamptey, a youngster from Ghana. Jean raved about him. Nii was really brought to Anderlecht on his recommendation. I had nothing to do with that, I was not asked about it. The club just got him, but I thought it was fun and interesting. That boy stood out during that youth World Cup and Anderlecht could perhaps use him in the future.'

Nii: 'My first encounter with Anderlecht was with a youth team, on 18 August 1989. I had just been in Belgium for a few days. It was at Neerpede, the youth complex, and everyone from Anderlecht was present. Keshi was there to guide me, and Michel Verschueren was there. Of course, he wanted to make sure I was the real Nii Lamptey, although Keshi had already emphasised that at the airport. But after that first training, he definitely was convinced! That training was accompanied by a lot of publicity. Everyone wanted to see my first practice.

'Meanwhile, the club also arranged language lessons for me, both English and French. Very nice, because I had a hard time speaking English when I was just in Belgium. I had never spoken French before, and I also had trouble solving easy calculations. I could speak a little bit of English, but I couldn't read and write well. I had to learn English at school but I didn't go often. I could still write my name but writing a whole story about myself was difficult. At home I didn't speak English, but Ga. I belong to the Ga, one of the dozen ethnic groups in Ghana. So I was happy with the language lessons I got; they helped me a lot. That is one of the reasons that I am still very grateful to Anderlecht. Especially the English lesson was very important to me. As a result, other things, such as learning to express myself well, also became a lot easier. I was taught three times a week, two hours each time. The beginning was quite difficult but of course I had little choice. But at some point it got easier. I was surprised about that, because of course I wasn't used to many classes. In any case my English improved quickly; at a certain point I could also speak a word of French. So I only really learned to master English in Brussels thanks to those lessons, even though English was also spoken in Ghana.

'When I was in Belgium for a few weeks, the weather slowly started to change. It was autumn and starting to get colder. I thought it was getting grey and boring. I was not used to the cold and had never seen snow. The weather was the only thing about Belgium that I didn't like. In the end, that was nothing compared to the things from my childhood, so I could deal with it.

'But after a few months I suddenly had enough of everything. The weather, the culture, the food; I suddenly really wanted to go back to Ghana. I couldn't take it anymore. But Keshi told me to hold on, that I would make it. Shortly after my arrival in Belgium I thought the same. The culture was so different that I soon wanted to return to Ghana. I was there on my own as a youngster; that was difficult. But even then Keshi supported me and said it would be OK and that I should stay. He convinced me twice to stay. Without him I would have gone back to Ghana long ago.

'Incidentally, it was not only Keshi who helped me in Belgium. Everyone at the club supported me. Michel Verschueren, Constant Vanden Stock, Aad de Mos and the technical staff, they've done a lot for me. Even Monique, the washer woman. Anderlecht has made me the man I am today.

'Meanwhile, playing football in the youth team went well, fortunately. The club was also satisfied. And suddenly I got used to everything, from one moment to the next. That was very strange, but nice. I ended up staying with Keshi and his wife for about three months. In that environment it was a lot easier for me to get used to Belgium. After all, I was still young and, moreover, alone, without family. And I ended up in a completely different culture. When I finally got used to everything I left for a host family, near the stadium. I would live there for the foreseeable future. More youth players from the club lived in the area, also with host families.'

Verschueren: 'After a few months Nii was placed with a host family in Brussels. That was different then than it is now. We had a few families back then who hosted youth players. They were friends of the club and people whom we trusted. They liked doing that and they were often older people. Now everything is much more organised. Back then everything was a little looser, a little more spontaneous.'

Lucy van den Borre was working in the clubhouse of Anderlecht at the time: 'I was still at secondary school but had a part-time job at the club. I helped make food and drinks in the clubhouse and with the waiters. That's how I quickly got to know the players, including Nii. Because I worked there, I also got a season ticket, so I could follow the matches. So, I grew up with Anderlecht. I also lived near the Neerpede training complex. I could be found there regularly; later I also went to away games. As a result, the bond with the club and some players became closer and closer.

'At the time, Anderlecht worked with all kinds of host families where youth players could stay. Those players came from afar and they couldn't go home every day. During the week they were taken care of in host families, on the weekends they had competitions, and afterwards they often went to visit their parents. Some guys, like Nii, couldn't go home for a while, of course. He didn't have a home in Belgium like others had. But he was well taken care of, everyone knew his situation. That's why we often spent time together on weekends. Nii would sometimes talk about the past, but not much. Never really about family matters, and when he talked about the past, it was often the positive things. He never spoke about all the negative things. I don't know if he just wanted to put all that behind him, but he is a positive person. He always sees the good in things and people, even when things are not going well.'

Nii: 'From my host family I walked to the training complex before every training session, about a 30-minute walk. By now it was winter, and I was walking through the cold every day, regularly seeing players who were dropped off by their families or who came by car themselves. That made me sad sometimes because I had no family in Belgium. But also because I had to walk. That didn't go unnoticed at Anderlecht either. People from the club took me to Eddy Merckx's bike shop, where I was measured, and a bike was adjusted for me. From now on I could go to training on a racing bike. That bike was later stolen. But then Anderlecht bought me a moped. So, from now on I could go to training on a moped!

'After the season with the youth team of Anderlecht, Aad de Mos allowed me to train with the first team quite regularly. I still remember my first day. It was around the birthday of Aad de Mos, at the end of March 1990. They wanted to do something fun. I was put in a big box and they put a blanket over it. The box was then presented to De Mos as a birthday present. He pulled the blanket away and there I was, in that box, as a present for De Mos, to indicate that I was the present, for his squad!'

Chapter 5

Success at Anderlecht

FROM THE 1990/91 season I became a permanent member of Anderlecht's first team. I trained regularly with the team in the last few months of the season before, but that summer I was moved up. However, my debut would be a few months later, which was no problem because I was only 15 years old at the time. But I loved that I was now officially in the first team.

Aad de Mos took good care of me. It's difficult to describe him as a trainer. I saw him mainly as a father figure, not as a coach. The difference with Stephen Keshi was that he was more of a role model for me as a footballer, and an advisor. So those are two different things. When I was having a hard time, and when I had to cry, I could go to Keshi. Aad de Mos was more the father who wanted his son, me, to succeed. They were both very important and helped me succeed at Anderlecht.

Besides Stephen, there were also a few other guys who were very important, for the team but also for me personally. Marc Degryse was important to the team and also to learn from. He advised and gave tips. The same was true for Luc Nilis. But I could also learn a lot from Luís Oliveira, Filip de Wilde, and Charly Musonda. I also mainly dealt with the younger players – Johan Walem, Bertrand Crasson, Pär Zetterberg and Philip Osundu – boys who also came from the youth, and with whom I'd already played together there. Big names that I wouldn't soon forget.

Some players got mad at me during training. That happened especially in my early period at Anderlecht. I was very fast so sometimes I wanted to slalom through everything. As a result, naturally I would sometimes get kicked. Or someone put me in my place or tried to challenge me. Those were the consequences but I also accepted that. It was part of a learning process, as hard as that may sound.

The same summer that I was transferred to the first team, there was even more good news. Mister Michel came to me and asked if there were any other players in Ghana who were as good as me. I said, 'Mister Michel, even better players?' He looked at me surprised, 'Are you sure, Nii? Who then?' At that moment I considered: who could make it in Europe? There were several good players in Ghana.

But now that I knew a little about football in Europe, I was able to make a reasonable estimate of who had the best chance of success. I mentioned the names of Yaw Preko and Isaac Asare. Preko was an attacker with a good pace, and Asare was a defender with a good overview of the game. Verschueren replied, 'Nii, you are very good. Are you sure they are better than you?' I repeated that they were both better than me, not knowing that at that time someone else had already tipped him off about two Ghanaians – Asare and Preko.

* * *

Verschueren: 'Yaw Preko and Isaac Asare also came to Anderlecht from Ghana after Nii. Not in the special way that Nii did, but in the normal way, as transfers usually should go. Preko was a good player, really. He played here for a number of years, until 1997. Asare also stayed until 1997 but he played very little here. Jean Pierre Kindermans, a scout at the time, made those transfers possible.'

Preko: 'When we went to that youth World Cup in 1989, nobody was really thinking about a football career. It was especially exciting for us because none of us had ever been to Europe. Nobody thought about the idea that you could make football your job. In Ghana there were two big clubs: Asante Kotoko and Hearts of Oak. If you wanted to make it in Ghana, you had to join one of those clubs. After that World Cup I ended up at Hearts of Oak as a youngster. You could not achieve more as a Ghanaian footballer at that time. At least that's what I thought. And that wasn't even about the money because you didn't earn much there. But when Nii left for Europe, the realisation slowly came that there was more than just these two clubs out there. That we could also go abroad.'

Nii: 'It was about one or two weeks after Mister Michel asked me about Isaac and Yaw. I was with my host family, and I was sleeping. It was still early in the morning when suddenly there was a knock on my door. I had no idea who that could be so early. A little annoyed, I got up; I opened the blinds and then saw a cheerful Yaw and Isaac standing in front of my window. I couldn't believe my eyes. When I saw them at my window, I hadn't seen them in almost a year. Since I arrived in Belgium, I had not yet been back to Ghana and therefore also not to the Ghana under-16s.'

Preko: 'We hadn't seen Nii in a long time, so of course he was happy that we were suddenly in front of him. He knew that Anderlecht was interested in us. They had asked him about Isaac and me and he was positive about our coming to the club. Isaac and I started in the youth, while Nii was already training with the first team. Nii guided us a bit in the beginning. That first week we saw him train with the first team, at the Neerpede training complex, he seemed to have become a completely different person! He looked nothing like the boy who left Ghana the year before, and I mean that in a positive way. He was, of course, only a boy, but a boy who was still growing physically. And the difference was clearly visible. He had gotten a lot stronger. When we saw Nii train there, Isaac and I also realised: this is it. This is real life. We are in the process of being a part of it. Nii was the example for us in this. A couple of guys coming all the way from Africa and trying to make it here. Life in Africa and thus also in Ghana was a lot less comfortable then than it is now.

'We were well looked after in Brussels. We got training gear and shoes, and were able to follow good training sessions. That was not the case at all in Ghana. Even at the national team there was no uniform then. Everyone just wore their own clothes. Isaac and I didn't know anything about Belgium when we got there. We arrived in the Netherlands sometime in the morning, with a KLM flight. From there we still had to travel to Brussels. Everything was arranged by Anderlecht and Jean Pierre Kindermans. He came to Ghana to arrange everything for our trip to Belgium, including our visas. We had to do that at the

Belgian embassy in Togo, because Belgium did not have an embassy in Ghana. We had to go to Togo first to apply and then come back later to collect our visas. But he had a good time in Ghana. He arranged everything perfectly for us.

'We were well received upon our arrival in Belgium. Several host families lived around the stadium, where youth players were housed. Nii lived there somewhere, as did Pär Zetterberg and Philip Osondu. The club arranged all of that. Shelter and food, but also a good salary. But that didn't matter then. We only thought about football. I know I moved to Anderlecht for about $80,000, Nii for $100,000. I don't know about Isaac. That amount for Nii wasn't bad, not for someone who played in the Cornerstones youth team. I came to Hearts of Oak after the World Cup in Scotland. They reasoned that if I could hold my own at a youth World Cup, I would also be good enough for the competition in Ghana. Isaac ended up at Cornerstones, the same club Nii came from.'

Lucy van den Borre: 'The youth players who didn't go home at the weekend were left alone in Brussels. So were Nii, Yaw and Isaac. We often went to the Westland shopping centre, and I often went to the cinema with them. They had plenty of time to do those kinds of things anyway. For example, they weren't indoors with their host family all day. Nii was an open and jovial person, very friendly. He had no allures at all, which you see a lot in boys of 16 and 17 years old these days. As we got to know each other better, he also came to our house. Every Sunday afternoon he came by at some point, along with Preko and Asare. They came to eat chicken with us. Every Sunday, that had become a habit with us. By the way, they ate every part of the chicken, including the cartilage. We are still talking about that.

'Nii was not shy, but sometimes naive. He had little life experience. He suddenly got to know a lot of people, and of course everyone thought they meant well for him. But he came here from Ghana at a young age. Then it is difficult to know who to trust and who not. He may have trusted people too quickly and too easily. But he was extremely friendly. He always took the lead when he was with Preko and Asare. Asare was quite accommodating, and Preko was very cheerful, a bit of a joker. They looked a bit up to Lamptey I could see. But Nii had been in Brussels for some time. He showed them around the city a bit.'

Preko also remembers the trips to Westland well: 'Westland! We were at home there. We always went there to the Quick, a snack shop, eating chips and chicken. Another store we often stayed at was the music store. We sat down to listen to music and buy CDs. And cassettes! Sometimes we bought blank cassettes or videotapes. Then we recorded music from the radio or video clips from MTV. We would then send them back to family and friends in Ghana, and we would have something to play when friends came to visit us.'

Nii: 'We regularly bought CDs with African music, such as Papa Wemba, who has since passed away. Music was and is a great support to me, I love it. I have a lot of friends, but music is one of them.'

Preko: 'Just like with Nii, Stephen Keshi was also important to Isaac and me. We saw him there as a father figure. Above all he taught us what we had to do to succeed, but also to remember where we came from. The pressure on us from Ghana was great; also, from friends and family. Stephen taught us to deal with that. He also taught us to enjoy everything. We used to visit his house regularly. His wife treated us like her own children. We all came from Africa and that creates a bond. They would cook for us, and sometimes we babysat their children.

'In addition, Keshi was a big name throughout Africa as the captain of Nigeria. We looked up to him as youth players. The great Keshi who helped us make it in Europe! That's why we listened to him. He was our point of contact in case of problems. I remember a moment when we stood with him at the entrance to the stadium, ready to enter.

He told us that someone had taken us to Anderlecht, but if we didn't perform, they would drop us just as easily. They would then just bring in someone else. We had to remember that. I still remember the exact spot where we stood when he gave that advice. He said we had to compete with a lot of white players, and if we played equal, the club would probably be more likely to choose a white player. So, we always had to give it our everything, be disciplined and try to convince the club to choose us. He passed that on to us.

'Jean Dockx had already seen Isaac and I play at the World Cup in Scotland. When I ended up at Anderlecht a year later, we sometimes talked about the World Cup and Africa. I always gave him a very polite answer. According to Jean, that's why I should have become a lawyer! He liked to tease me. Then he talked about that tournament in Scotland, and how innocent and timid we were then. We walked with our heads down the whole time at that World Cup, very modestly. But I would say, "Of course we did. We came from Africa, where all the football fields were brown with dry grass. We had never seen green grass before. But in Belgium it is normal. Here the grass is green everywhere. So now I'm walking with my head up, because it's not special anymore!" I am very sorry that Jean passed away so early.'

Nii: 'The story is that I signed my professional contract with Anderlecht when I turned 16, on 10 December 1990. A wonderful birthday present, it was argued. But in fairness, I must say that is not my date of birth at all. It's actually 30 December! Everywhere it says 10 December, also in all kinds of documents that have been drawn up over the years. Something went wrong somewhere. Perhaps with the translation, that they did not understand me correctly or that they copied or typed something incorrectly. As a result, an error has crept in. But I used to not worry about things like that, partly because I didn't see the importance of it. And I've never had any problems with it, so I just accepted it, I just didn't want to get into trouble. So, I never brought up about that date being wrong. That is why 10 December is considered my date of birth everywhere. But officially it's 30 December! So, I actually signed my professional contract when I was 15, a few weeks before my real birthday. But on paper I was 16 at the time. From that moment on I could play for Anderlecht. Two days later I was already sitting on the bench for the first time, during a match in the UEFA Cup. It was an away game in Germany. We lost to Borussia Dortmund, 2-1, but that was just enough to get to the next round, as the first game was won 1-0.

'A few days later, on 15 December 1990, I made my debut for Anderlecht. In the away game against Cercle Brugge, I replaced Luc Nilis after 32 minutes. My debut turned into a dream when I also scored. Of course I was happy; you don't forget such a moment quickly. In those moments I felt in everything that the misery of my youth had not been in vain. Strangely enough, I also remember that I was on the field with Dutchman John van Loen. To this day, I am the youngest-ever goalscorer in the Belgian league. According to the record, I was 16 years and six days old. But because my real date of birth is 30 December 1974, there are 20 days to take off. So actually I was 15 years and 351 days old! So I was just 16 on paper when I made my debut, but not everyone believed that.

'Apart from the date of birth, which was incorrect, people have often asked me about my age – whether I really was the age that was written on the paper. It was also a common problem back then; in the past it was much easier to tamper with. Some footballers have admitted that after their careers. But I get it, because it's just a way to market yourself better and to escape life here. And perhaps the football associations arranged all this themselves because they also benefit from it. By arranging a new age for players. We heard those stories too. Not only in Ghana, but it also happens in many other countries. And of course, some people thought I'd lied about that too. But when I came to Belgium I was really 14 years old. I was growing and trained a lot at Anderlecht. I wasn't used to many physically demanding training sessions, and I was also going through my puberty. So, I grew quite a bit during that period, and because of those training sessions my muscle strength also increased.'

Verschueren: 'I've always assumed that Nii was as old as the age stated on his passport. I had no reason to doubt that, but I couldn't anyway. And he played in Ghana's under-16s, so you assume the age is right. In any case, I could not imagine Nii being older than stated in his passport.'

Nii: 'In April of 1991 I was called up to the Ghana national team for the first time. It came as no surprise to be honest. I felt I was ready for the next step. After all, I had already played a youth World Cup and had made my debut at Anderlecht. At Anderlecht Mister Michel and Aad de Mos came to me at one point and congratulated me. They said that Anderlecht had received a phone call informing me that I had been called up for the Ghana national team. Not much later, an official letter followed. I then joined Ghana in a team with some big names, including Tony Yeboah, Abédi Pelé and James Kwesi Appiah. Burkhard Ziese, a

German, had been appointed coach at the beginning of that year. On 29 April 1991 I made my debut in a qualifying match for the 1992 Africa Cup of Nations. It was against Togo, which took place in Kumasi.

'We won that game 2-0, and just like with my debut for Anderlecht, I also scored on my debut for Ghana. I scored to make it 1-0. That was of course very nice and, in any case, it was a good feeling to play for your country at the highest level. I was proud, I wanted to represent my country as often as possible. On the other hand, I must conclude that that attitude is partly the reason that my career at club level started to falter a few years later. I wanted to play everything for Ghana, I was called up for everything. Even if the football association couldn't or wouldn't pay for my plane tickets, I still went to Ghana and paid for the tickets myself. I started with Ghana under-16s, but then also played in the under-20s and under-23s, the Olympic team. And, of course, the Black Stars. That was not a problem at Anderlecht, because I didn't always play there. It wasn't until a few years later that it really became a problem and my club career started to suffer.

'After my debut in December 1990, the rest of the competition went very well. I scored regularly and started playing more and more. I played in 14 league games that season, and once in the cup. In March I also made my European debut for Anderlecht, an away match against AS Roma. They lost 3-0, and two weeks later we also lost the home game 3-2. I still managed to score in that game. On 11 May we played our championship game against RWDM. We won 1-0 just before time was up, but I didn't play that game. But of course I was very happy because we had become champions. It was nice to win my first prize with Anderlecht after such a great season. We celebrated in the Jacuzzi and in the dressing room, there was champagne, and overjoyed fans rushed on to the field. They tried to get our shirts and even hung on to the goals. It was fantastic. So far, my career has gone very well.

'So it was only a matter of time before I got an agent who could represent me and manage my affairs. Eventually that became Antonio Caliendo, an Italian. I met him for the first time at Anderlecht, sometime in 1991. At that time there were a few agents who wanted to take me under their wing: Caliendo, Domenico Ricci and someone else. In the end I chose Caliendo. At the time, he was one of the largest agents in the world. He had players under his wing such as Roberto Baggio, Dunga and Salvatore "Toto" Schillaci. He promised me that I would immediately receive money from him if I signed with him. He also said that he would take me to Italy in the future, to a big club, although I don't remember if he mentioned names. He told me that then I would earn twice as much as now. It was never my dream to play football in Italy, I didn't have a specific club or even country in mind. In my teens I hardly knew anything about football in Europe. I knew nothing about Spain, France or Italy. At the time I only knew Liverpool from Europe, with John Barnes and Ian Rush. English football was sometimes shown on television in Ghana. But otherwise I hardly knew European clubs. I waited where fate would take me.'

Lucy van den Borre: 'In 1991 Nii met Antonio Caliendo. Nii would sign a contract with him, making Caliendo his agent. Sometime in the middle of the week they had agreed to sign that contract, somewhere in a hotel in Brussels. He would do that with Caliendo and a lawyer from Italy. Nii asked if I wanted to come along. He liked it when someone else would be there, someone he knew. He told me he was going to sign a contract and then maybe he could play football in Italy. He would also receive money, he said. I decided to go with him.

'Nii came to pick me up at home, and a large white limousine with a driver was parked outside the door. That agent arranged that. With that, we drove to that hotel where we met Caliendo and that lawyer. Caliendo explained extensively about Italy. He promised Nii to take him to a big club there. To AC Milan or Internazionale, I don't remember. Nii also received a cheque for 300,000 Belgian francs on the spot, now about €7,500. He picked up that cheque, casually folded it and tucked it in the back pocket of his trousers. I asked Nii what he was doing. He didn't know that piece of paper was worth money! I told him to take it to the bank so they could put the money into his account. We did that the next day. He had no idea about such things. In that respect he was easy to manipulate, people could quickly trick him into anything. Caliendo and that lawyer didn't care. Nii was given no explanation as to what exactly that cheque was and what to do with it, while they should be the people who should pay attention to that. But if Nii had lost that cheque, he could never have cashed it. And they probably wouldn't care.'

Nii: 'I don't know exactly what was in Caliendo's contract. It was difficult to read, and everything was described so difficultly that I often didn't know what certain things meant. But out of good faith I just signed. In retrospect that was very naive. But Caliendo also made no effort to explain exactly what it said and what it all meant. Since I was still a minor, he also needed the signature of my parents, or at least one of them. Caliendo therefore went to

Ghana to get written permission from my father to become my agent. My father then gave Caliendo a power of attorney to manage my financial affairs on my behalf from then on. I had no insight into that, I also don't know what exactly my father signed. I have no idea how my money was handled during that time. I received an amount every month, I knew nothing about the rest.'

Verschueren: 'From the moment Nii signed with Caliendo, things started to go a bit wrong. Then he slowly started to distance himself from the club. You saw him break away from Anderlecht. Nii had faith in us and the club at first, but that has turned blindly into confidence in Caliendo. He approached Nii, and Nii signed a contract with Caliendo. He wanted to take Nii to the top, or so he said. Caliendo thought he had a new world star in his stable. He firmly believed in Nii's class. That man promised him everything, placated him with expensive things. But that was of course also in his own interest.'

Nii: 'I had been absent from Ghana under-16s for over a year. Sometime in the first half of 1991, the team reunited to play a number of qualifying matches for the U-16 World Cup. In qualifying we narrowly eliminated Sierra Leone and then Guinea. Then Morocco were disqualified after our first match, which we won 2-0. So we qualified again for the under-16 World Cup, in which I was still able to participate that year. Preko and Asare also played again.

'After my first season in the first team of Anderlecht I felt very strong. I had made my debut at Anderlecht and played regularly since then. I had scored seven times in the league, plus another goal in the UEFA Cup against AS Roma. And I had made my debut in the Ghana national team. But there was not much time to reminisce. The youth World Cup was to take place in Italy that summer, but before that we usually went to a training camp for a few weeks, this time in Germany. Our trainer at the time, Otto Pfister, was from there. We then flew from Germany to Italy, where the World Cup started in mid-August. Pfister had become our coach for Ghana under-16s in 1991. He was very strict, very disciplined. We had to do everything according to his rules. If he told us how to play football, we did. But we were also easy to coach. He was a beloved coach.

'In Ghana people are in awe of the elderly, and often learn things from them. Young people listen to what they say. That was also the case with Otto Pfister. And I'm sorry to say it, but even then we had the perception that white people were "on top of the world". That's why we were happy that he was our coach. And he had many years of experience in African football. He ended up working for the Ghana

Football Association for a few years. He also became the coach of the Black Stars in 1992 and even became African Manager of the Year.

'By the way, his style of dressing became fashionable in Ghana. He sat on the bench during matches, but with his trousers always so low on his hips that you could see his boxer shorts. Sometimes you could even see the top of his butt! That then became fashion in Ghana. A lot of people then started wearing their trousers in the same way. That was then called "an Otto Pfister". This is a well-known phenomenon to this day. Some schools banned that way of wearing trousers, always referring to an "Otto Pfister".'

Preko: 'Pfister was not too positive about the way Nii had left Ghana. He coined the word "kidnapping" because Nii hadn't been allowed to leave the training camp. Moreover, he had entered Belgium illegally. That could not get Pfister's approval; he was also a man of discipline and rules.'

Nii: 'The mentality in the team was different compared to two years earlier. We were all two years older and meanwhile I was now a professional football player. Together with Preko and Asare, who both played in the youth of Anderlecht, we were the only players from the team who played football abroad. And we came back a lot stronger and better.'

Preko: 'Our team-mates also saw the difference. We wore new clothes and new shoes. From that moment on you saw the mentality of many boys change. We were the centre of attention and that was when many players realised that maybe they could do the same.'

Nii: 'But the atmosphere was no less. We were like family. That's what I remember most about that tournament. That's why we were so hard to beat. So, president Rawlings's decision to confiscate all our passports two years earlier was not such a bad thing in hindsight. After all, the team remained intact, and that contributed to our success that tournament.'

* * *

We started the World Cup well. In our first game we played against Cuba. I was captain and scored twice, once from a penalty. We won 2-1, then Uruguay followed. That was a very hard match. They tried to intimidate you, some even spat. I was also booked in that game. Fortunately we won 2-0, and I scored again. In the last game we drew 1-1 against Spain, who had a strong team. But, at that time, Spain and us had both already qualified for the quarter-finals. We had to play against Brazil and knew we would have a hard time. Before we went to the stadium, we already packed our things. We had been told that, if we lost, we would immediately fly back to Ghana. However we won 2-1, and I managed to score again. Back at the hotel we could unpack our things again. We then saw the Brazilians leave. They were in the same hotel as us.

In the semi-finals we had to play Qatar, who had beaten the United States in the quarter-finals. People sometimes talk about African players who cheat with their age, but those Qatari players were no better. How strong and big those boys were! The score was 0-0 after extra time. I got a yellow card in this match after eight minutes. We only managed to beat them 4-2 on penalties, where I scored the first.

In the final we met Spain again. We were not reassured; we were very nervous actually. Pfister told us not to underestimate Spain. They were good and could win the game. But, he said, 'We need to tap into our African forces.' Those kinds of things helped us. Pfister often knew exactly what to say to us. He had many years of experience with African teams and knew how players sometimes thought. Once on the field there were all kinds of emotions: tension, but also joy that we were there. It was all very strange. We were already happy to be present at a World Cup again, but now we were in the final and eventually won it 1-0 with a goal from Emmanuel Duah.

After everything I had been through as a child, this was a dream come true. There I stood. From the boy who never went to school to world champion with Ghana under-16s. All the misery and pain of the past seemed to be paying off. At that moment I forgot everything from my past. After we finally ended up in the dressing room, we stayed there to celebrate, shouting, singing, dancing, but also praying and thanking God. It went on and on; unbelievable. It took a while before we got out of the locker room. And yes, we had a good team, but to win that tournament, that was something! And that wasn't just for me personally. This was fantastic for the whole team; everyone should be proud.

After the celebrations and festivities in the stadium, we drove back by bus from Florence to our hotel in Montecatini. When we got there late at night it was very busy. There were all kinds of agents around, and of course you can guess why. At that time I already had a contract with Caliendo so I was no longer interesting to them. Other players, yes of course. There were also many fans of Ghana in attendance, Ghanaians who lived in Italy and came to congratulate us. They were also frantic. We got presents from them and they sometimes gave us money. And they gave us food! Typical Ghanaian dishes, such as jollof and kenkey. Apparently they thought we missed that there. And they were right! It was all very nice. Everyone was ecstatic in Ghana, but also the Ghanaians abroad.

The tournament was also a personal highlight for me. I became the top scorer with four goals together with Adriano from Brazil. He was eventually awarded the Golden Shoe because he had played fewer games. However, I was crowned the best player of the tournament and received the Golden Ball for that. By then I had already been crowned man of the match four times, so that prize was already on its way. Several of our guys were named man of the match: Isaac Asare, I think, Mohammed Gargo too.

After the World Cup, Yaw, Isaac and I returned to Belgium. We didn't go to Ghana first. It would have been illogical if we first went to Ghana from Italy. Unfortunately we missed the entire folk festival. We found that quite difficult because we wanted to go back to Ghana with the team. They were received as heroes. They also toured through Accra, which was logical, because it was the first time that a representative team of Ghana managed to win a world title. That's why the championship has not been forgotten to this day. But we were also professionals. We were now playing football in Europe, that was the most important thing. So we went straight back to Brussels from Italy, also because I was already in the first team and the competition had already started. A few years after that tournament, a major road past the national stadium in Accra was named after our team that won the World Cup: The Black Starlets '91 Road. What an honour!

Fortunately, when we returned to Belgium, we were also well received by everyone. A few people from Anderlecht were waiting for us at the airport, dressed in traditional African dresses. Beautiful. President Rawlings was extremely proud of the team. Later we visited him in Accra. There we handed over the trophy to him. To our surprise, each player also received five million cedi, which was about $500 at the time. We had to put the money in a savings account because we were still minors. We couldn't have it until we turned 18. I know that almost everyone took their money straight from the bank once they were 18. I kept my money for a while and later spent it on my first child.

After my first season in the first team at Anderlecht and the youth World Cup in Italy, I had apparently also been noticed by a few people at Adidas. They offered me a great deal that summer and I signed a five-year contract with them. The money I got for that was huge. That was only the first time I really realised that there was a lot of money to be made with football. So, from then on, I wore their clothes, shoes and tracksuits, also at home and even in the pool. I saw myself on posters and every month I got new stuff. I couldn't believe it at first. A young boy from Ghana who was featured on Adidas posters in Belgium. Every month I was called and went to their office where I tried on all my clothes. They put everything in a big box, and it was delivered to Anderlecht. I took a lot of that stuff with me when I went back to Ghana. There I gave those things away to friends and acquaintances, so that they could also benefit from it. So for me it was a big deal, a dream. It was the only sponsorship deal I ever made in my playing career. After I finished playing I teamed up with a few companies in Ghana, who used me in their marketing campaigns.

When we returned to Belgium after the World Cup, the new season had already started and unfortunately Stephen Keshi left Anderlecht for RC Strasbourg in France. Yaw, Isaac and I had to do without him, but by now I had been in Belgium for two years so I already felt at home there. Adri van Tiggelen and John van Loen had also left, and Pär Zetterberg and Philip Osundu had been loaned out. On the other hand, John Bosman and Danny Boffin, among others, had joined us, players I would also receive a lot of support from. Because of the World Cup I had already missed the match for the Belgian Super Cup, which Anderlecht lost. Four rounds had already been played in the league competition and after my return I was to continue playing football straight away, but I didn't mind that I didn't play much in that early stages. It went well in that first half of the season with the team, and in the winter break we were at the top. In November and December I was back in the starting line-up several times and scored again. We were eliminated early in the cup, but we were still active in the European Cup. On 12 December I was allowed to play my first European game of the season, against Red Star Belgrade. However, because of the war in what was then Yugoslavia, we played that match in Budapest. I scored the equaliser to make the score 1-1, but in the end we lost 3-2.

In 1991 it had been a very busy but important year for me. And, from a sporting point of view, it was also a wonderful year. At the end of 1991 I came fifth in the African Footballer of the Year competition, an award that then went to Abédi Pelé. At the time the award was still organised by *France Football* magazine. I was not present at the awards ceremony, but I heard afterwards that I had finished fifth. It was fun because I was still very young. And the names ahead of me me, there was no shame in ending up behind them. Behind Pelé, George Weah was second, François Oman-Biyik third and Kalusha Bwalya of PSV fourth. I only turned 17 at the end of that year and came in fifth! The magazine *Afrique Football* also held a similar vote, in which I even came third, behind Pelé and Weah. It felt like acknowledgment that all the misery from my youth had not been in vain.

I thought about that a lot during those years. It was a challenge for me not to fail, but I gladly accepted that challenge. I wanted to succeed because of everything I had already experienced in my youth. I was mistreated, blamed for everything, I was ignored, and that was largely because of football. That's not fun being a kid. I had hardly been a child. So, all those things that happened so early in my football career, I was and still am immensely grateful for that. I put a lot of pressure on myself, but I still do today with my school, with my football academy. In Africa sometimes people like to see others failing so they have someone to point to, to laugh at. For that reason alone, the pressure to succeed is great.

After the turn of the year, the second half of the season would start the same for me as the first half. I again had to miss a few games for Anderlecht because of the Africa Cup of Nations that was held in January. It was Ghana's first participation since 1984, but expectations were very high. That team is known as one of the strongest African teams ever – and maybe it was. From the youth squad that won the World Cup six months earlier, Mohammed Gargo, Isaac Asare, Yaw Préko and I were now included. Abédi Pelé and Tony Yeboah were the big players then, while we also had other veterans in the team with James Kwesi Appiah, Stephen Frimpong and Anthony Baffoe. And players like Ali Ibrahim, Prince Polley and Sarfo Gyamfi had also played in Europe. However, there were also some tensions within the team at the time. There was some disagreement between Yeboah and Pelé in particular. It was explained as a tussle between the Ashanti, to which Yeboah belonged, and the Ga, to which Pelé belonged. Both had support from a few players, which seemed to create a bit of disunity in the team. But I didn't engage in that discussion. I was young and had no say, so I kept my distance. In the end our football didn't suffer because we did make it to the final.

Despite our selection, it was a tough tournament because there were a few good teams. Moreover, a lot of physical football was played; it was different than in Europe. I had to get used to that a lot. And it was my first Africa Cup of Nations. I was extremely nervous, especially for the first game. It was so bad that I vomited blood on the field. It looked black. That was against Zambia, a game we won 1-0. But at that time there were more things going on. So maybe that was reflected on the field in that blood vomiting.

Maybe I was too stressed, because at that moment everyone wanted something from me. The pressure was high; I played a lot of games for someone who was just 17. That vomiting happened a few times during that period, but it didn't stop me from playing football. Sometimes I think it was also because someone wished me something bad, a curse. In Africa, many people believe that they can be cursed by someone. I believe that too when I think about all those things that happened in the past. But luckily God is on my side; that's why I'm still here. Fortunately, in the matches after that I managed to control my nerves. After Zambia we also beat Egypt 1-0, both strong countries at that time. We then defeated Congo 2-1 in the quarter-finals.

In the semi-finals we played against Stephen Keshi's Nigeria. It was a lot of fun playing against him, of course, but Nigeria and Ghana are big enemies when it comes to football. We quickly fell behind, but thanks to goals from Abédi Pelé and Prince Polley we won 2-1. Unfortunately Pelé got a yellow card in that match, and because he already had one he was suspended from the final. And he was our most important player at that time. He had already scored three times in that tournament and was the African Footballer of the Year. He was at the peak of his career at the time, playing for the great Olympique Marseille side.

A lot depended on him during that tournament, so we were disappointed that he was not allowed to play in the final.

In the final against the Ivory Coast we drew 0-0 after extra time. In the end we lost the penalty shootout 11-10. I scored my penalty, and it was unbelievable that our entire team had to take a kick. In the end Asare missed, but then the Ivory Coast did too. The rest of the players from both teams all succeeded in their turn. That had never happened in a major tournament. Because everyone had already taken a penalty, we had to start all over again. Anthony Baffoe, who had already taken our first penalty, ended up missing our 12th, after which Ivory Coast scored and won the cup. In the end a silver medal was not bad, but with this team we should have won. I could be satisfied because I played a good tournament. I didn't score, but I played all the games.

After the final we returned to Belgium; Isaac, Yaw and I, but also Prince Polley, who played for Germinal Ekeren at the time. I had already missed three matches for Anderlecht and I didn't play the following three games either. Then I played regularly again until the end of the season and scored another goal against Germinal Ekeren. Unfortunately we lost leadership to Club Brugge a few games before the end. Then we drew against KV Mechelen, which put Bruges further ahead. Because we then lost the second-to-last game we could no longer finish above them. In that respect 1992 was the year of not quite: I came in second with Anderlecht and I lost the final of the Africa Cup.

In the summer of 1992 I had to play another big tournament. With Ghana's under-23s we had qualified for the Olympic Games in Barcelona. The Olympic team was led by Sam Arday, a very funny man; you could laugh a lot with him. He hardly ever called anyone by their real name and always gave everyone nicknames. He sadly passed away in February 2017.

We had qualified relatively easily for the Games. In the first round the best countries were given byes, including Ghana. When we had to play against Guinea in the second round they were suspended and so we were already in the third round without playing. We had struggled against Sierra Leone before, and did this time too. At home we won 2-1 but away we lost 3-2. We therefore qualified for the last round, in which we had no trouble with Mauritius, winning 6-0 and 4-1. Mauritius were very weak but they had benefited from a walkover against Zambia and the Ivory Coast in both the second and third rounds.

Despite the fairly easy qualification, we thought it was an honour because playing at the Olympics was not something that could be taken for granted. In my opinion the atmosphere was slightly better than the year before at the youth World Cup. Our Olympic team was one of the most special and crazy teams in Ghana I played in. We were just having fun. It went very well with most players, many of whom now played abroad. That was a huge difference from a year and a half earlier and we were satisfied. The atmosphere was good, we all went shopping together, that sort of thing. And this also fitted into my career at the time. I was satisfied, everything went well, people knew me; I had little to complain about at that time. Unfortunately I also had to deal with setbacks at that tournament.

The first game went well, we won it 3-1 against Australia. However, two days later, in our match against Denmark, I injured my groin. That was right at the start of the game, I was replaced by Yaw Preko, and in the end we drew 0-0. I had a lot of trouble; I couldn't really play again in the tournament but it was expected that I would do, so I tried to play the game after that, despite the injury. I skipped the training sessions to relieve my groin and I just played the games. I got a few injections for every game to ease the pain, but it always came back twice as hard.

Two days later we were in action again, and with a 1-1 draw against Mexico we still managed to reach the quarter-finals, albeit with difficulty. Three games in five days is not nothing. We had an extra day of rest before the quarter-final against Paraguay and it was difficult for them too. We led 2-0, but Paraguay came back to equalise and in the end we won 4-2 in extra time.

In the semi-finals we faced Spain. That was a very good team, including Albert Ferrer, Pep Guardiola, Luís Enrique and Abelardo. I faced Guardiola in that match and Spain were a bit too good at that time. We lost 2-0. Two days later we played against Australia again for third place. Australia missed a penalty early in the game, and shortly afterwards Asare scored from a free kick to make it 1-0. At the end of the first half my injury really became unbearable. I had already received a yellow card. My groin was really hurting, and I just had to be replaced. Luckily it stayed at 1-0 and so we won a bronze medal! Some people expected nothing less than a gold medal, but we were very happy with bronze. I didn't feel like there was more in it for us this time. Spain won the gold, but it was well deserved. It was Ghana's first Olympic medal outside of boxing, and the last medal to date.

It was a wonderful feeling to win a medal at the Olympics because for Ghana it was very special. Until then, only three medals had been won over the years: one silver and two bronze. So we had delivered a good performance in that respect, and we were also the first African country to win an Olympic medal in football. That was something to be proud of.

Chapter 6

The last season in Belgium

JUST AFTER winning the bronze medal at the Olympics, Isaac, Yaw and I came back to Anderlecht. Just like the previous season, the league competition had already started so I had again missed part of the preparation and the first game. But what was more worrisome was that I came back injured. I had been playing with injections for almost the entire tournament so that I wouldn't feel my groin injury, but that made the injury worse. I spoke honestly to Anderlecht about what had happened, and they were very angry. I was out of circulation for four months because of that injury and therefore missed almost the entire first half of the season.

When I think about it now, I didn't take good care of myself back then. I was young and had never learned to deal with injuries, and I always just wanted to play football. I didn't know what was and wasn't good for my body.

* * *

Yaw Preko: 'Maybe Nii felt physically tired at times, but still had the intense need to be on the field. That he had to prove himself on that field, no matter how he felt. But he also felt happy there. It was difficult to slow him down, he always wanted to play. And when he played, he gave 100 per cent. He struggled to temporise a bit now and then, to also take rest while on the field. But that summer he started having problems with his groin. I think he was overloaded then. But he wanted it so badly, I think he ignored it. When the Ghana Football Association called him, he always went. He was always on the field, whether that was with the first team, with the second team or on the training field. But if you're not fit you can never give 100 per cent. So it came at the expense of his game. But he was young, had had few injuries until then and hadn't yet learned to deal with injuries.'

Nii: 'Besides that injury, something else had happened that summer that had an influence on the new season. Aad de Mos was fired. I remember crying when I heard he was leaving. Aad de Mos was important to me, he trusted me. He meant a lot to me. I don't know how to thank him. He was like a father to me.'

Michel Verschueren: 'Aad de Mos was fired after the 1991/92 season. He's always been a bit of a spectacular man. He was demanding, but he also had his quirks. He sometimes tried to excite players by tarnishing them a bit in their honour. That started to get on the nerves of some of the players, and the results in his last season were also disappointing. So psychologically he was "special". But I always got on well with him, it clicked. At some point, however, the board decided to break it off with him. A year later he ended up at PSV. After his dismissal there, the manager of Werder Bremen called me, I gave De Mos a good recommendation at that club and he went there. It didn't last long, though.

'De Mos was succeeded by Luka Peruzović, but that didn't work either. He wanted to be in training camp before every game. But at those training camps, he was constantly in his room. He only joined the team to eat, and to have a brief discussion. Then he went back to his room. The players were irritated by things like that and they showed that to us at a certain point. We then decided to stop with him, even though we were first in the competition. At the time this unleashed quite a smear in the Belgian media and the board received a lot of criticism. He was then succeeded by Jan Boskamp, who then became a three-time champion with Anderlecht.'

Nii: 'The rest of that season did not go well at Anderlecht. And I really don't even know how that was possible either.

Perhaps the departure of De Mos had to do with that. He was so important to me! He really had a great effect on me and, when he left, that feeling wasn't there anymore. I didn't seem to be able to take that extra step anymore. And his successors also had a different way of playing, that also had to do with it. First came Luka Peruzović. He was still quite young, but straightforward. But I think Anderlecht was just too big for him at that time. The pressure there was always very great. But I actually had very little contact with him. I was injured of course those first months and in January he was fired.

'Then came Jan Boskamp. He was also completely different from De Mos. His training methods, the way he would speak, he came across as much more aggressive. Maybe he thought players were too lazy, that they needed to be dealt with. It always seemed that way. But that didn't work for me. I was not feeling well because of my injury and the departure of De Mos. But Boskamp was not a bad trainer, he had his heart in the right place. He could also be very funny.'

* * *

After my injury I could finally make my comeback for Anderlecht at the beginning of January. In the home game against SK Lommel I came on for Alain Van Baekel about 20 minutes before the end. That was nice. A few days later,

Peruzović was fired and we continued with Jan Boskamp. As I started to get fit again I was called up again for the Ghana national teams. The under-21s (now the under-20s) had qualified for the Under-21 Africa Cup, at that time still called the African Championship. I was only just fit again, but of course I wanted to play for Ghana. Those kinds of moments were not pleasant because I had to make a difficult choice. I decided to go anyway, but that was at the expense of my career at Anderlecht.

In the African Championship we were in a difficult group. We started with a narrow win over host country Mauritius, but then lost 2-0 to Cameroon. In a head-to-head game for a spot in the semi-finals, we defeated Nigeria 1-0 and then in the semi-final we defeated Egypt 3-1 after extra time. In the final we faced up against Cameroon again, but this time we won 2-0 and so I took another prize, which was quite nice because those months before had been very frustrating because of my injury. And with that win, we automatically qualified for the U-20 World Cup in Australia. That was in March 1993, so that month I could hardly play for Anderlecht. But of course I also wanted to go to the World Cup.

Anderlecht were criticised for that because it seemed as if I could never play for the club, 'only' for Ghana, especially as in April I started having problems with my knee. I was called up for an international match against Germany, but my knee didn't feel right. I then had to undergo exploratory surgery in Antwerp and was again out of circulation for a few weeks, even though there was nothing seriously wrong with my knee.

Having won the African Championship, we travelled to Australia with a very good feeling. And just like in 1991 I was captain there too. Isaac Asare was also present. And with Daniel Addo, Samuel Kuffour, Charles Akonnor, Emmanuel Duah, Augustine Ahinful and Mohammed Gargo, among others, we were there again with a good team. I think I was the only player who already played in the Ghana national team at that time. I was very busy with all those obligations and during that time I didn't even play in the first team at Anderlecht.

The tournament went very well, but we didn't win in the first two games. We drew 1-1 against Uruguay and 2-2 with Germany, so we had to win our last group match against Portugal to advance to the next round. Fortunately I scored after five minutes and Akonnor made it 2-0. Then the quarter-finals went pretty well and we beat Russia 3-0. We had a harder time against England in the semi-final but we won 2-1 and were again in a final.

We played against Brazil in the final and took the lead early on, but we had a very hard time with them. Shortly after the break they equalised, and a few minutes before the end they scored again to make it 2-1. But both goals came after a foul from them, one on me and one on Mohammed Gargo. There was no whistle, and they then scored in the attacks that followed. I was white-hot with anger. I blamed the referee afterwards for our defeat because he didn't whistle for those fouls. But of course that didn't help. I was really disappointed. I cried; everything went through my mind. For a moment I even thought he was whistling on us because we were black, things like that. We may have won a silver medal but I didn't feel good about it at all.

At the tournament, another strange occurrence took place. It was the only time I experienced anything like it. Before the match with Russia in the quarter-finals, an Asian man approached me and offered me $10,000 if we lost. Of course I knew that wasn't allowed, and I didn't go into it either. But I was a bit shocked. I kept it quiet and didn't really know how to handle it at the time. Later I told my team-mates what had happened. Years later, some people have doubted my story. They thought I had accepted that money because eventually I could afford just about everything I had ever wanted. But of course that wasn't the case. I wouldn't just betray my country.

When I came back to Belgium after that tournament, Anderlecht did well. Boskamp therefore saw no reason to put me in the starting line-up. That switch worked out well for Asare and Preko, who both made their debut in the first team under Boskamp. Unfortunately I didn't play for the rest of the season. We became champions that year but I hadn't really contributed. The same was true for Charly Musonda. He had been injured a lot that season so also didn't play a lot. But more importantly, he was still alive. Man, Musonda was lucky that season. I'm very glad he's still alive.

* * *

Verschueren: 'Musonda had been injured a lot that season. Sometime in April, however, he was invited to an international match for Zambia. He came to tell me, but I said I didn't agree. He wasn't allowed to leave me because I thought he had to get completely fit first. He really wanted to join the national team, because they had to play an important qualifier for the World Cup. But I just said "no". I kept him in Brussels. On 27 April the plane with the Zambian team, without Musonda, flew from the Zambian capital Lusaka to Senegal. It was a small plane and would make a few stops, but after the second stop in Gabon it went wrong. The plane crashed into the Atlantic Ocean shortly after take-off. All 30 people on board, and therefore the entire squad, were killed. Musonda would have been on that plane otherwise. Because I wanted him to stay in Brussels because of that injury, he escaped that fate. Captain Kalusha Bwalya played for PSV and escaped that disaster in a similar way. To this day Charly is grateful to me for that, although it was of course a coincidence. It did, however, create a special bond and we are still in touch regularly. Friends for life, that's what he calls us.'

Nii: 'After the U-20 World Cup in Australia, I had to report to the Ghana national team again not much later. It was around one of those matches that I met Gloria. We were in a hotel somewhere in Accra when Tony Yeboah called me in my room. His girlfriend had come to the hotel and brought a friend, and she wanted to meet me. Tony's girlfriend then introduced Gloria to me, and we clicked. I brought her home later that night, and we've kept in close touch ever since.'

* * *

At Anderlecht I had hardly played in the first team that season, because I was away a lot with Ghana but also because of my injuries. I couldn't really join the team for a season. And we had become champions. Why would Boskamp change the team then? I didn't get the feeling that my situation would change at Anderlecht the next season either. It seemed rather hopeless. But to be honest, I was also ready for a new step in my career.

Fortunately, Anderlecht were open to a transfer at that time. At that time I had already played for Anderlecht for more than three and a half years, a long time. I met many good players there, but it is difficult to single anyone out. You wouldn't be giving the other players enough credit. And I also felt at home in Brussels. I can still hear the fans shouting my name in the stands. The only other place I experienced that was some time later in China.

* * *

Preko: 'A lot of good players were around at Anderlecht, but if there was one person who was important to the team, it was undoubtedly Marc Degryse. When I came to the selection, I looked up to him a lot. He was a real number ten. He really saw everything. All you had to do was just move around the field. When he wasn't playing, you noticed something was missing. When he later left Anderlecht, Pär Zetterberg took his place. I played well with both players, but Degryse – he was special.'

Nii: 'At that time, I was not in Boskamp's plans. The club was willing to let me go for the right amount. They were asking a lot of money, and maybe that deterred clubs. PSV from the Netherlands were also interested. That summer, Aad de Mos was appointed there as a trainer, and of course we already knew each other.'

Chapter 7

Top season at PSV

ANTONIO CALIENDO had already mentioned Italy, but apparently there were no Italian clubs at that time willing to put the desired transfer amount on the table. Napoli and Lecce had been in touch with Anderlecht but had not taken any action. A year before, somewhere in February 1992, Juventus had spoke to Anderlecht. Then, converted to today's money, I would have cost about five million euros. At the time that was a large amount. I didn't have a specific country in mind that I really wanted to go to.

* * *

Aad de Mos: 'I'd only signed a contract with PSV on 21 June, and the squad would already meet for the first time on 5 July. The preparation time was therefore very short. Contrary to my appointment at Anderlecht, I didn't have months to focus on the team, but just under two weeks. Far too short, in my opinion. I saw that first year mainly as a build-up year for the following season. I was given far-reaching powers on a technical level, although that did not immediately have major consequences for the group of players. But I was also given a clear task: I had to clear the rubble.

'The season before, things had gone wrong on several fronts. The championship was wasted in the final phase of the competition and there was a fuss with Romário, the absolute star. In his last two seasons in particular he regularly caused discord in the squad. Some accepted his antics off the field and his slack attitude during training simply because he was a footballer of the highest calibre. The rest of the squad, however, was greatly disturbed by this. As a result, groups were formed in the team and that did not benefit the atmosphere.

'At PSV you also had the remnants of the group that had won the European Cup in 1988: Hans van Breukelen, Berry van Aerle, Edward Linskens, Wim Kieft, Jan Heintze, Gerald Vanenburg. They had won everything there was to win. And there was unrest because of the call to bring in young blood and thin the team. The squad was so large that we sometimes had to divide it between two dressing rooms during training sessions. That was not conducive to the atmosphere. It had to be fixed. A unity had to be forged again.

'When I signed my contract, Hans Westerhof, my predecessor, Erik Meijer, and the Swede Klas Ingesson had already signed up. But those weren't players that made me feel hot or cold. There would be no more financial room for reinforcements unless more players left. It soon became apparent that Romário would leave, because he was nowhere to be seen at the start of the season. It was a loss, but better for the team. And Gerald Vanenburg also left the club. So suddenly there was money available to get a few more players. On the day that Romário signed with FC Barcelona, Edwin van Ankeren signed with PSV. I remembered him from my time in Belgium, he came over from RWDM. In addition, I also wanted to attract a creative, attacking player. Romário left a big void in that regard. That's when I started thinking about Nii. At Anderlecht, Nii got sidetracked after I left. He did not play under Peruzović, and after he was fired, also not under Boskamp. But I thought he was a good guy and I thought he was a good candidate for a reinforcement for PSV. I knew him, I knew his qualities.

'I wasn't sure if Lamptey was the player we were looking for at the time, but I didn't have much time to do an extensive search. He would therefore first come on a trial basis at PSV. On 20 July I was able to take him and see him at work in a practice match, but then he was slightly injured. A few days later he was in action again, in a practice match against FC Antwerp. He scored both goals to make it 2-2. We decided then that we wanted to loan him, but Anderlecht didn't want to even consider that. They were clear: Lamptey is only for sale. But buying was not an option for PSV due to the high transfer fee. PSV could not or did not want to cough up that amount. We couldn't figure it out and Nii returned to Anderlecht. But just under two weeks later, Anderlecht were suddenly willing to talk about a loan and the clubs quickly settled the matter. Apparently they couldn't sell Nii for their asking price. This was good news for us because the competition was about to start.

Nii: 'Everything felt different at PSV from the start. PSV was a bigger club, and the level was higher there. The difference with Anderlecht was big altogether. Anderlecht's squad was good, but this was a more mature team, with more older guys. In my opinion they were slightly ahead of Anderlecht. Of course, I was happy that PSV wanted to take me for at least one season. During my first training in Eindhoven I immediately wanted to show too much – dribbling, scoring; at least, that's what De Mos thought. He told me to take it easy. I didn't have to prove anything to him, he already knew me. I adapted quickly in Eindhoven, although it helped that Aad de Mos was a trainer there.

Luckily, I was able to communicate with everyone in English. In Belgium I sometimes had to speak French and that was difficult.'

* * *

In Eindhoven I lived in an apartment near the stadium. I didn't know the city yet, so I often went back to Brussels. That wasn't that far away. I liked that, because that was familiar territory for me, and I knew people there. So after competitions I often drove to Brussels. But I also loved the Netherlands, I can't really explain why. I loved it in Eindhoven. A big city, but also quiet. There was a lovely Chinese restaurant there that I often went to eat at, I've forgotten the name. I also often went to a Philips store there to buy electronics.

At PSV I also occasionally spent time with a few boys outside of football, with Kalusha Bwalya, for example, 'King Kalu'. I already knew him; he was a big name in Africa and captain of the Zambian team. He was important to me at PSV. He gave me advice and I listened to him. He had the same luck as Charly Musonda a few months earlier as he still had club obligations at PSV when the rest of the Zambian team died in that plane crash. I also listened to Erwin Koeman a lot; he was important to the team. Klas Ingesson was also new to PSV that season. He was a nice guy from Sweden. He was in very good shape. I occasionally hung out with him, just like Tom van Mol. They also came from abroad and that created a bit of a bond. And Robert Fuchs and Arthur Numan were also young, I used to hang out with them a bit also.

You also had a group of older boys. Gheorghe 'Gica' Popescu was a little shy, but very funny. He could really make you laugh. Jan Wouters came to PSV during the winter break but I don't think I ever heard him talk! He seemed shy, but defensively he was strong. He was very good. There were also Wim Kieft, Jerry de Jong, Berry van Aerle, Jan Heintze, Gregory Playfair. I remembered Adri van Tiggelen from my Anderlecht days. And Hans van Breukelen of course. You could always hear him yelling in the games. But one day, the way he lashed out at me was exceptional. I never experienced that again after that. He literally made me cry; I will never forget that. During a match, I can't remember who against, Gregory Playfair was about to score. The ball rolled towards the goal line but I was already running in that direction and gave it one last tap with my foot at the end, so the goal was given in my name. Van Breukelen was furious in the break. He was really raging at me in the locker room. I just gave that ball an extra tap so that a defender who was close by could not reach it anymore, but Van Breukelen just yelled and scolded me saying that I was selfish, that I just wanted to score myself. I felt very sad. Kalusha then took me aside for a while.

* * *

De Mos: 'Van Breukelen was always acting up. I was aware of that. Eric Gerets and Søren Lerby used to mess with him, and he would not open his mouth. When they left PSV, Van Breukelen tried to take over their leadership role. After 1988 he'd been honoured for the prizes won and his penalty saves against Benfica [in the 1988 European Cup Final] and the Soviet Union [in that year's European Championship Final] and then he took on a certain role. He would rant against youngsters or new boys but tried to remain friends with important boys like Wim Kieft and Arthur Numan. That was typical of the "schoolteacher" Van Breukelen. I once said to him, "I don't think you're a good keeper at all. I think you're a made keeper. I only know one keeper who has everything by nature and that is Michel Preud'homme. I think that's the best goalkeeper in the world. So, you just have to act normal." He could never appreciate me telling him that. He knew that I had brought Nii to Eindhoven and he then attacked Nii. That was typical of Van Breukelen.

'Before matches, he often hung up pieces of tape. He needed it for his fingers because he had already broken several of them. Then when he went to the bathroom or talked to someone, other players quickly took that tape away. He was often messed with. At the end of his career, he was busy with lectures. We'd have an afternoon off and he had planned such a lecture. During lunch I played with the players for a while and told the group that I'd changed the whole schedule and that we'd train that afternoon after all. A joke, of course, but Van Breukelen was completely stressed. At the end of lunch, Van Breukelen would ask if we could talk and that he had a problem with that afternoon. Those boys already knew what was going on and would be rolling on the floor laughing.

'I saw a very different Lamptey at PSV that season. He also realised that something had to be done after his last season with Anderlecht. He had lost his flair and confidence. His development had come to a standstill. Fortunately he knew what was being asked of him. During training sessions he put in much less effort than at Anderlecht. However, he sometimes still had to be reminded of certain tasks. Don't let his man run away, for example. Nii got on well with most guys. He kind of became the darling of the group. Everyone liked him. He got along particularly well with Kalusha, who took Lamptey under his wing a bit in Eindhoven.'

Nii: '[Sunday] 15 August was my debut at PSV. Three games later I scored my first goal for PSV, an equaliser against Willem II. After that I started to score with some regularity, including against Feyenoord. The highlight was my two goals against Ajax, a match we won 4-1. In the end I scored ten times in 22 league games that season. Together with Arthur Numan I'd even become the club's top scorer. So, for me personally it was a very good season, but at PSV they were not satisfied with the results of the team. They were too inconsistent and there was unrest among the players, but I didn't notice much of it myself. For me that situation was less important as a loan player. At a certain point I knew that many players had to leave Eindhoven after that season and were in uncertainty, but I didn't think there was a bad atmosphere in the squad. I think the problem was that there were relatively many older players around. The balance was lost. Those players had already been through and won everything: Van Breukelen, Koeman, Linskens, Popescu, Van Tiggelen; some players had to find out about their departure from the newspaper. That wasn't good for the club.'

* * *

In March 1994 a list of names of players who were to leave Eindhoven was leaked. It contained 14 names, including Lamptey. Old-timers Van Aerle, Kieft, Van Tiggelen, Heintze, Erwin Koeman and Van Breukelen were also on it, along with Juul Ellerman, Kalusha, Jerry de Jong, Wim de Ron and Gica Popescu. The signings from the previous season, Edwin van Ankeren and Klas Ingesson, would be leaving too, having not made a great impression. It upset several players who heard the news from the media. They accused chairman Maeyer of sitting in the manager's chair.

Nii: 'I went back to Ghana in mid-March. I was called up to the Ghana national team, with whom we went into training camp for the Africa Cup of Nations, which was to start in Tunisia at the end of that month. So, I had to leave PSV for a few weeks. Unfortunately it was not a memorable tournament. Qualifying was already strange because Tanzania and Burkina Faso withdrew from our group, so in the end we only had to deal with Liberia, against whom we won twice. At the tournament itself, we won 1-0 against Guinea and Senegal with a lot of effort, but then in the quarter-finals we lost 2-1 to Ivory Coast and the competition was over for us after three games. That was quite a disappointment, especially after our success two years earlier.

I knew that I had to leave PSV at the end of the season. That was made clear to me at the beginning of March. PSV weren't going to buy me, but I didn't want to go back to Anderlecht either. Jan Boskamp was still the trainer and my position was not so good there, but I could have done something about that myself by playing well and not getting injured, and being present more often. But the main reason was that it felt like a step back, and I didn't want that. At PSV I had made a step forward and I wanted to continue on that line. Going back to Anderlecht wasn't a step forward for me.

* * *

Preko: 'We were happy that Nii was able to play again at PSV. We were proud, and happy, that he could show it again. You saw that Nii was fit again and was therefore a much better player than he had shown in his last season at Anderlecht. I think Anderlecht also realised that they had to let Nii go.

The Dutch league was still more highly regarded than that of Belgium, and Nii showed that he could join PSV. PSV had hired him, however, so he returned to Anderlecht after that season. But you could see he didn't feel like it. He wanted to go higher.'

* * *

I also kept in touch with Gloria at PSV and, in the meantime, we would also speak of a relationship. I didn't see her often, but when I was in Ghana I would visit her. She wanted to visit Eindhoven one day. I was fine with that, so I contacted PSV and they arranged everything for her. Not much later she came to the Netherlands for three weeks. Of course, I had to train and play football, and at those times she was home alone. She would cook for me when I went home between training sessions; she would prepare typical Ghanaian dishes. But in practice nothing came of this. When I came home, she often had nothing prepared, while I didn't have a lot of time. The only thing she sometimes prepared were fried bananas. So I went to get Chinese food at my favourite restaurant.

But despite that, those three weeks were still enjoyable. It went so well that we decided to get married. But not without reason: Gloria was now pregnant with our first child. We actually wanted to get married before our child was born. A fairly traditional idea, which is now also a bit outdated, but I didn't know any better at the time. And I was famous in Ghana, so you want to do what you think is best. I informed my family that we were planning to get married and that Gloria was pregnant. From that moment on, some things changed. When it became clear that Gloria was pregnant and we were getting married, my mother let me know that she didn't think she was a good woman for me. She was against marriage. But I was young, I had money; I didn't listen to my mother. Not even when it came to Gloria. What could my mother do about it? We decided to get married that summer, in Ghana, on 28 May 1994, just after the season. Gloria arranged all that because I was in the Netherlands at the time.

It wasn't much, we just registered as husband and wife. Nothing else, so there was no big wedding party or anything like that. A few weeks before we got married, however, Latifah was born. We were very happy and had a big party in Ghana. We celebrated that in a big way, unlike our wedding, which was more of a formality.

I invited Alhaji Salifu Abubakar to attend our wedding. I regarded Salifu as a father. He had trusted me and had given me shelter. But he didn't want to come; Salifu was also not happy with Gloria. He didn't support our relationship, let alone our marriage. I was surprised, but it turned out that Salifu had found out that I had brought Gloria to the Netherlands. That wasn't a secret, but I hadn't told him. That wasn't necessary either. He was angry that I had brought Gloria over when I didn't even know her very well. But Salifu mainly felt that he had more right to come to the Netherlands first. He thought I owed him a lot and that I should have let him visit first. He thought I should have even invited some guys from Kaloum Stars. But love is different from friendship. I felt bad about that because I thought his opinion was important. He could have just said that to me. But instead, he said things behind my back to others, like, 'She's not a good woman, she's going to cause trouble, Nii deserves better.' He said things like that. I learned about that from other people. But he didn't know her. He was mostly jealous.

I also noticed other strange things. During my time at Anderlecht, I had a house built in Kumasi, where I let my father live. That despite what he had done to me in the past. He was able to live there with my stepmother, who had actually been responsible for me having to leave their house. And when my father got a little older, he stopped working as a car mechanic. I also bought him a car at the time because he wanted to become a taxi driver. Then he could earn something extra, and he also had something to do. If I was in Ghana now and then, I also stayed in that house, because it was my house after all. It was only at those moments that I got closer to my father, but also to my three half-brothers. I'd never experienced that before because they were very young when I lived with them in Kumasi.

That house was built next to Salifu's house. But when we got into an argument, I noticed that there were all kinds of things around and even in my house that had to do with black magic. Apparently, there were people who tried to influence me like that. That scared me. And because I was also angry with Salifu, I decided to leave that house and buy another one. My father and his family continued to live there. I thought it was pretty bad because I also supported the children who walked around Kaloum Stars. Later I found out that he actually wanted me to marry his sister. But I was already in love with Gloria.

Chapter 8

Aston Villa

I WAS not happy when I left PSV. Anderlecht's asking price for me was too high and PSV were not going to pay it. That summer I returned to Ghana, where I stayed for about a month. Then Antonio Caliendo called me to tell me that he had found me a new club: Aston Villa in England. I didn't really know the club, all I knew was that they had brought in some new players. But I quickly resigned myself to moving. I thought Caliendo knew about that sort of thing, and I had to report to the club a week later. In retrospect I should never have made that step to England. I had to change my playing style a lot and the country was not suitable for me. I should never have done it. I went to England at the wrong time.

* * *

Michel Verschueren: 'We always had good contact with Aston Villa. Maybe that's why Nii went to that club, I don't remember. That contact had been there since 1982, when we played the semi-finals of the European Cup against Aston Villa. When we played there, I got the idea of skyboxes. We then introduced the idea to Anderlecht as well during the renovation of the stadium in 1983.'

Nii: 'On 10 August I signed a contract with Aston Villa. For me, signing a contract was a formality. I assumed Caliendo was handling all business things properly. I didn't even think about it because I just wanted to play football. The rest didn't interest me. Caliendo had already arranged everything before I got there. I signed at Aston Villa what he had agreed to with the club. I really don't know the details of the contract, but they weren't explained to me. I know my salary was going up at the time, so I just trusted Caliendo.'

* * *

Pelé's words from a few years earlier still played a role. That never really went away, even when it became clear that I could never match him. I still remember going to my hotel room when I first arrived in England. It had just been announced that I had signed with Aston Villa. I turned on my TV and there was a football programme on. In it, someone said that Pelé's successor would come to Aston Villa. As a result I hardly had time to adjust. I was expected to be there right from the start and to also perform as Pelé had. So there was that pressure there too. I could handle that, but of course it wasn't fair to make that comparison with Pelé.

In England, I especially had trouble with the language at the beginning. The English that was spoken there, with that typical accent, I found difficult to understand. I had to ask quite a few times what was being said, but then it just continued in the same way. They spoke quickly and I had to make an effort to understand them, but eventually I kind of got the hang of it.

The Villa team I ended up in was a great group. I have to smile when I think again about that team from time to time. A good team, despite the disappointing results that season. We had a large group of black players at Villa. John Fashanu was the craziest one there. One evening he came by my house. He had rented a limousine to go out with all the black guys! He wanted all of us to go to a nightclub together, so he came by to pick everyone up: Dalian Atkinson, Dwight Yorke, Ugo Ehiogu, Ian Taylor, Bryan Small, the whole group. But I never liked it that much. I wasn't a clubbing type. I didn't go many times, but I always thanked them kindly for such invitations.

In addition to John, Dalian Atkinson and Dean

Saunders were also great fun. They could put a smile on your face. They were always arguing with each other about the craziest things. I also remember the rest of the team well: Phil King, Franz Carr, Gary Charles, Graham Fenton, Michael Oakes, Tommy Johnson, Andy Townsend, Dean Saunders and Mark Bosnich from Australia. He got on well with Dwight Yorke and was often at his house. I lived near Yorke at the time. I liked Steve Staunton too, he was a solid defender. And Paul McGrath; I thought Paul was a very smart player. The same was true for Dean and Dalian. Dalian sadly passed away in 2016. According to his family, he was depressed, partly because of heart and kidney problems. He was not himself and, in a kind of psychosis, had attacked his own father. The police came and tasered him, after which his heart gave out. CPR was to no avail. And unfortunately Ugo Ehiogu is no longer here either. He died in 2017 after a heart attack at Tottenham Hotspur's training ground.

Since I had arrived at Aston Villa late in pre-season, it took until 21 September for me to make my debut. We played against Wigan Athletic in the second round of the League Cup and won 5-0; I scored once. From then on I played regularly. Three days later I also made my league debut as a substitute against Blackburn Rovers. A few weeks after my first match we played the return against Wigan in the League Cup. We won 3-0 and I scored twice. I then played with more regularity in October.

Then, in November, something happened that I would be reminded of for years to come. That month we played against Tottenham Hotspur, where the German Jürgen Klinsmann played at the time. At one point I ended up in a duel with him, where his aluminium cleats on his boot made full contact with my knee. I was out of action for a few weeks, and in the years that followed I continued to suffer with that knee. Sometimes I didn't feel anything and everything went fine. But at other times I did suffer, and that ultimately hastened the end of my career.

Earlier that month, Ron Atkinson was fired as manager due to disappointing results and Brian Little then took over. At that time I was in Ghana for the national team. Later that month I had to go to Ghana again and was away for almost two weeks. In December I played for Villa again, but after that I was no longer in Little's plans. The fact that I had to report to the Ghanaian national team again in January didn't help at all, of course. Little did not give me a chance in the second half of the season.

After the winter break I only played for Villa's second team, 12 times, in which I scored three goals. Because I was away a lot my game was very hit-and-miss. If I had to go to Ghana for commitments and then come back, I always had to compete with someone in my position. The moment I felt I was winning that battle, I was called back to Ghana again. This of course didn't help me to become a real part of the team. But in the end I didn't fit into the system either. I was a player who liked to have the ball, and English football at the time was often still the old-fashioned 'kick and rush' style. Only the top clubs like Manchester United played quite differently. So I didn't like the game at all. When we were in possession I wanted to get the ball from our defence, but before I could even ask for the ball it had already been kicked forward. It was also very tough physically.

It was difficult from the start at Villa. The way they treated each other in training was fine, but there was also a lot of competition. It was quite a challenge. My input in the first team was ultimately limited to six league games, and three appearances and three goals in the League Cup. Because my prospects at the club were not good, my contract was terminated in mid-May 1995. There was no point in continuing on with each other any longer.

I was on a free transfer at the time. Ron Atkinson liked me, by the way, and I liked him too. 'Big Ron' was his nickname. He was important to me, I thought he was a very good coach. He also gave me advice on matters off the field. I learned years later that Atkinson had made a racist remark about French footballer Marcel Desailly, but I don't believe he meant it. It was probably more of a joke. It was a clumsy statement, though. He said something 'off-camera' and it happened to be recorded. Anyway, I don't take it too seriously.

Atkinson had been appointed at Coventry City, who also played in the Premier League. When I was told that he would like to take me to Coventry I didn't have to think twice. In retrospect I wish I had made a different decision, because it was also a lot of 'kick and rush' football at Coventry. I still struggled with the problem that I had to go back to Ghana regularly, and wanted to. The next season wasn't that different in that regard. I should have known better.

Chapter 9

Coventry City

DESPITE HAVING played little in the last six months, Ron Atkinson brought me to Coventry City. Ron knew me, and moreover the club didn't have to pay a transfer fee for me because I was a free agent. After everything was arranged and the contract was signed, I started training. After a few days Atkinson suddenly called me to him. He asked when I was coming to get my money. I asked, 'What money?' I knew nothing about money at all. It turned out to be the signing-on fee. Atkinson had to explain to me what that was; I didn't even know such a thing existed. I gave my account number to which the money was then transferred. The fact that I heard about that fee was purely coincidental.

Not much later, Antonio Caliendo went to the club to ask about the money. There he was told that Coventry had already transferred the money to me. Then he came to me to ask for that money. He said he needed it because he had to pay a few people who had also worked on the transfer. But according to Coventry, that money was mine. I discussed it with him for an hour. He showed all kinds of documents, but I knew nothing about them. Finally, he angrily threw those documents away and then ran away. He never saw that money.

Coventry's squad was modest, not hosting as many big names as Aston Villa. Notable were Sam Shilton and Peter Shilton, father and son. They were both there but neither played very much. Peter Shilton was a big name but he was past his prime. He left in the winter, but I still feel privileged to have been in the squad with him. Later I heard that he had gotten into financial problems due to gambling, among other things, but that he is now well again, fortunately.

I also remember Lorcan Costello, John Salako, Marcus Hall and Dion Dublin. I got on well with the last two. And there was Peter Ndlovu, from Zimbabwe. He was my room-mate at training camps. He was the first African in the newly established Premier League. And of course, I remember Kevin Richardson, our captain. He had a very aggressive way of playing. Then you had David Busst, a defender. He collided with two players late in the 1995/96 season against Manchester United, Denis Irwin and Brian McClair. David suffered a double fracture in his leg in what is considered one of the worst footballing injuries ever. There was even talk of the leg being amputated, but in the end that was not necessary. Unfortunately it marked the end of David's career. He did get a farewell match against United in 1997. That turned out to be Eric Cantona's last appearance; he suddenly announced his farewell two days later.

At Coventry, Big Ron had an assistant, Gordon Strachan, who was also a player at the same time. He didn't play much because of that dual role. Gordon would succeed Ron as manager the following season, as Ron himself would become director of football at the club. Gordon was already taking care of training. But one thing is certain, he and I didn't click. I don't know if he really hated me or if he was just being hard on me, but everything I did was wrong to him.

Nothing was right in his eyes; he couldn't be satisfied, until one day it got too much for me. It was the straw that broke the camel's back. He again let it be known that he was not satisfied with anything at training. I was furious and was about to hit him. Instead I ranted a lot at him. Apparently he was impressed, or had become afraid. For the next two days he was absent. He had never seen me like this. My team-mates eventually had to calm me down. Normally I'm very calm and can take a lot, but if you push me against the wall too much, well, that's human nature when someone goes too far.

At Coventry, the season started pretty well. My first two games were in the second round of the League Cup, against Hull City. At home we won 2-0 and I scored the opening goal, then away we won 1-0 – I also scored that goal. In mid-October I made my league debut, against Liverpool. Until November I played regularly, but in December that stopped. On New Year's Day I played again but after that I had to report to the Ghana national team ready for the Africa Cup of Nations in January 1996, which took place in South Africa.

Despite the tournament itself, I have fond memories of South Africa. It was a nice place. I went to a disco there once with the rest of the team. I calm never actually went out much, but after we won a match there we were all expected to go out together. I remember just sitting there somewhere, listening to the music. People were smoking and drinking. Tony Yeboah, who I got on well with, saw that I didn't feel at home there. I'm not a clubbing type, that's not my style. I don't smoke and don't drink, so I quickly went back to the hotel. I hardly ever went out with any of the clubs where I played. I'd rather have been at home watching TV or listening to music. My best friend was the music. People saw me on the football field but not off it. Even in between workouts I sometimes went home instead of going into town. It's just not me.

Meanwhile, Ghana's squad consisted of footballers who almost all played outside of Ghana. Of the 22 players, only five played in Ghana itself; quite a difference with the youth squad of 1991. After that year things went fast, and at the Africa Cup of Nations in 1992, 13 of the 22 players already were playing abroad. A lot had changed in a few years. I hadn't played much at Coventry that season and at Aston Villa the season before, but I didn't think that my position in the national team would be in jeopardy. But during the Africa Cup in 1996 I suddenly wasn't starting. In the first game I came on for Yaw Preko after the break, and in the end we won 2-0 against Ivory Coast. But I didn't play the next games. The Brazilian coach, Ismael Kurtz, came to me at one point, because he saw that I was surprised, and said, 'Nii, I'm sorry. But this is not my fault. I can't do anything about this.'

But I knew what was going on. There was a team-mate who no longer wanted to play with me at one team, Abédi Pelé. In Africa it often happens that players think that there is more at play with football than just what happens on the field. I'm talking about black magic, and things we can't control ourselves. He convinced the coaching staff that if I played with him, we would lose 'because our stars were in the same position'. I had to accept that, because I was younger than him. That's how it works in Ghana. In addition, he was also a big name in Ghana. It wasn't fun, but there wasn't much I could do about it.

We survived the group stage, also beating Tunisia 2-1 and Mozambique 2-0. In the quarter-finals we beat Zaire (now Congo-Kinshasa) 1-0. We were in the semi-finals, in which we had to play against South Africa. But Abédi Pelé didn't play, I don't remember why. But still I was not selected, so I was very angry. However, in the second half I was still allowed to come on. After about an hour I entered the field for Kwame Ayew, and we were already 2-0 behind. I was excited and full of fire. I quickly tackled someone from behind and was immediately sent off after being shown a red card. It felt really bad at the time, I can tell you. It was my low point with the national team. In the end, without me of course, Ghana played in the match for third and fourth place, which was lost to Zambia 1-0. When I returned to Ghana after the tournament, a journalist interviewed me. I'd had enough. I told him that for me that was the end of my career as an international for Ghana. It became a big issue and people even argued about it.

Strangely enough, I played one more international match after that, on 27 March 1996. Ghana had to play a friendly against Brazil. However, the Brazilian federation only wanted to play against us if Abédi Pelé, Tony Yeboah and I all participated, purely from a commercial point of view. That had already happened in a 1994 friendly against Japan. We were the big names then. So, given the interests, I had to appear. However, Abédi Pelé was absent, so I decided to play one more time. It was not a success and we lost 8-2 to Brazil against Rivaldo, among others. After 38 international matches and eight goals, that was the definitive end of my international career. I was only 21 years old and I've only once regretted my decision. That was a few months later, during the 1996 Olympics. Given my age, I was still able to participate in what would have been my second Olympics.

After the Africa Cup of Nations, I only played twice more for Coventry: once in the league against Middlesbrough and once in the FA Cup against Manchester City. When I wasn't playing, I was with the second team, just like other players who didn't get to play. There were always four or five players from the first-team squad. It was during this period that my father also passed away. He had started drinking more and more over the years, especially hard liquor. Once, when I returned from Europe, my father suddenly passed out during my visit. We immediately took him to the hospital. He'd been lucky; according to doctors he should have been happy that he was still alive and that I was around to take him to the hospital. At the hospital it turned out that his liver was too weak to tolerate any more alcohol. My father was then told that he had to stop drinking immediately.

But he couldn't. When I was there, he tried to slow down, but he only succeeded when I was there. I then tried to help him a little. I would remove the booze and buy him light beer instead. But as soon as I left, he started drinking liquor again. One day he wasn't feeling well, and his liver started to hurt. My half-brother Niiquaye, who still lived with our father, called me at one point and told me that he had passed away. The liquor had finally killed him. His liver was damaged from drinking too much. May he rest in peace. After the news of his passing, I went back to Ghana and arranged the entire funeral. In Ghana the eldest child is supposed to arrange that, so that's what I did. I paid for the entire funeral on my own. We buried him in Kumasi.

We used to never have that father-son bond. The basis for this was also missing. My parents separated, and when I lived in Accra, I never even saw him. Once I went to live with him in Kumasi I was not wanted and I was mistreated, which made me rebellious. But things changed when I played football abroad. By the time he passed away, we were getting along reasonably well, despite the things that had happened before. Our bond had changed. There was more understanding for each other's points of view. My father got older and milder, while I grew up and you just learn to understand certain things better. I now know that in the end he wanted the best for his children. He always put his children first, he himself came next. For example, if there was little food at home, he would feed us, leaving hardly anything himself. But as a child you don't realise that at all.

One of the last times I saw him, he wasn't doing well. Before going back to England I asked if there was anything else I could do for him. He then said that I had done so much for him. He didn't say he was sorry for all the things he'd done to me, but I could see he was. I believed what he said. Yes, he used to treat me badly. But it has made me strong. I don't blame him anymore. He appreciated what I had done for him. I let him live in my house, I bought him a car, I took care of him when I was there, even when he got sick. When I asked him if there was anything else I could do for him, he said he would like me to stop praying five times a day. I didn't promise him that at the time, but I eventually stopped.

The reason I stopped actively praying as a Muslim was mainly because the person who asked me to become a Muslim, Salifu, stopped supporting me. And I had mainly become a Muslim because at that time I was playing football at Kaloum Stars, an Islamic club. For me it was a matter of survival, that's what it came down to. My father was a little annoyed by that, but he finally knew why I did it.

Some people still think I pray five times a day, and others even call me by my Muslim name Abdul Nasir. But by the time my father died I had already converted to Christianity again. Ultimately I believe in one God, and one thing, 'do good'. That is the key to success. I'm not a big churchgoer and don't go every Sunday. I believe more in helping other people when I can afford it.

My stepmother also later apologised for what she did to me. But with her, it sounded like a lot of nonsense to me. She said it but I know when someone means it. She didn't mean it. That's why I didn't value it. It ended well for me, but what if something bad had happened? It wasn't really a thoughtless decision when she got me kicked out of the house. But later I let her live in my house with my father because at that time they had three children. She is now also deceased. Now I support my half-brothers who still live in Kumasi.

During my time at Coventry, my second daughter, Khadija, was born on 7 November 1995. Once a month we went to the hospital to make sure everything was going well with the baby and the pregnancy. One day I had just trained, and we had to go there again. At the hospital the doctor came to me to tell me that the baby had to be delivered by Caesarean section because she was so big. I didn't really understand that, but I was waiting in the hospital with Latifah, who was playing with a dummy. After an hour, Khadija was born. A few weeks later we had a whole ceremony for her birth, and I also invited my fellow players. I know Dion Dublin was there, but so was Tony Yeboah. He also played in England at the time, with Leeds United.

The second half of the season had been very hectic. I hardly played at Coventry, I had that hassle during the Africa Cup, the end of my international career, my father died and my second daughter was born. When the season ended I really wanted to leave, not just Coventry, but also England. It wasn't just because I didn't play much. Even if I had played a lot of football, I would still have wanted to have left simply because of the playing style there. I should have done that the year before. I don't think I was eligible for a longer stay either. I had to play a certain percentage of the matches there, otherwise my work permit would not be renewed. I was nowhere near that percentage so Antonio Caliendo had to put me in a new club again.

Chapter 10

To Italy, finally

BECAUSE I wanted to leave Coventry, Caliendo started looking for another club. He then came up with Venezia. In any case, he did what he had promised a few years earlier: he would place me at an Italian club. Logically, at the time he was talking about the big clubs – Internazionale, AC Milan, that level. But I signed for Venezia in Serie B, the second level, not what I had hoped for. Initially, after two years in England, Venezia felt like a kind of liberation, but unfortunately my time there was not a success.

Torino, another Italian club, had been interested in me. I learned that from Caliendo. But Abédi Pelé was playing there at the time. I used to consider him a friend, until the Africa Cup of Nations hassle. He told the coaching staff at Torino that I wasn't a good player and that I played like a small child. Just like he had done with the Ghana national team, he also told Torino that he couldn't play with me.

Partly because of that, Torino were no longer interested.

Caliendo was surprised, because Abédi and I knew each other. He told me what Abédi had said about me at Torino. I never asked Abédi why he did that, only God knows. But I know he has done that to other Ghanaian footballers as well. He left Torino that same summer. I actually didn't want to mention his name. When I do that, those bad memories come up. It hurt a lot, even today still. He had a big influence on my career in a negative sense. But most of all it hurt because I thought he was a friend. I showed him my respect, and he repaid it in this way. It was very painful. Abédi in Ghana was someone like Lionel Messi and Cristiano Ronaldo are today, a superstar. Maybe he didn't want to be in the shadow of another Ghanaian footballer so everything had to give way, even though we used to play together in the national team. Instead of destroying them and saying bad things about them, he should have welcomed the new generation. All that drama just because he apparently wanted to be in the spotlight on his own.

I was very surprised when I arrived in Venezia, a tourist town. I'm also not surprised that the club has hardly played in Serie A. That would be totally unsuitable. But the location of the stadium was fantastic! It was practically on the sea. I lived on the mainland, near the training complex. Then when I had to go to the stadium, I parked my car somewhere near the water, after which I continued from there by boat to the stadium. That first time taking the boat I found very scary. I also always put on a life jacket when on the boat, and after matches I also had to take the boat back to get to my car. That was unbelievable, so unique. It was so different from what I was used to.

Venezia wanted to move up to Serie A, so they had bought a lot of new players. Almost the whole squad was renewed. I was the only foreigner at the club and the rest were Italians. I don't have a clear memory of many players. I remember Simone Pavan, a defender. Claudio Bellucci was a striker who later left for Napoli. And I remember Cristiano Zanetti who was loaned by Fiorentina to Venezia. I got on well with him. We went for lunch regularly. That didn't happen to me often, because otherwise I found the Italians rather reserved. They were very private. Even in England people were much warmer and much more social. I felt lonely in Italy, even though Gloria and our children were there too.

At Venezia there was enough money, but there was no football sense. Things there were not going as they should. I didn't know anyone from the management, I never spoke to them there and that should tell you something. But the tactic of buying many players didn't work. In August we were already beaten in the Coppa Italia, the Italian cup, and our coach Gianfranco Bellotto was fired after just a few games. The results were disappointing, at least enough to cost Bellotto his job. But he was the person who took me on. Two other coaches, Walter De Vecchi and Franco Fontana, then took over. That didn't work out well for me. They brought their own players to the club and that was at my expense. I didn't get to play anymore and in the winter break I was to leave again. I wasn't counting on that. It became clear that they had no idea what they were doing at Venezia when both coaches were fired later that season and Bellotto came back again.

So once more Caliendo had to find me a club. At that time Palermo, who also played in Serie B, were interested. So I went there to talk to them, along with Caliendo. But I heard a lot of bad stories beforehand, including that the Italian mafia had ties with the club, and I didn't think it would be wise to go there. Not joining was a good choice because at the end of the season Palermo were relegated to Serie C, the third tier.

I found the country of Italy and the city of Venice very beautiful, nice people too. But Venice is a tourist destination and you shouldn't go there for football. In the end there was no second Italian club, but a team from Argentina were interested: Boca Juniors. Caliendo spoke to them, and I didn't have to think twice about Boca Juniors, a big club, where one of my idols played football at that time: Diego Maradona. We decided to travel directly to Argentina.

Chapter 11

Grief in Argentina

I DIDN'T think it was that strange that I left for Argentina. Boca Juniors were a big club known in Europe. I really didn't feel obliged to stay in Europe, so why wouldn't I head out there? I just didn't expect that flight to take so long! That was almost a reason for me to give up playing in Argentina. However, when we arrived in the country and spoke to a delegation from Boca Juniors, it soon became apparent I wouldn't be able to play for them for the time being. The problem was that that club already had four foreign players under contract that season, the maximum allowed number. A contract could therefore not be signed even though they were interested, so it would be a different Argentinian club for at least half a season. That became Unión de Santa Fe. If I did well there I might still have the chance to leave for Boca. I thought that really was a shame, especially because Diego Maradona was playing for Boca at the time. It would be a dream if I could have played with him, but that season turned out to be his last as a player. I was equally happy to be in Argentina, the land of Maradona. I was the first player from Ghana to sign for a club in the Argentinian league.

The league season was already halfway through when I got there, and it resumed at the end of February 1997. It was a tough competition and as a foreigner I really had to get used to it. Precisely because of that physical aspect, there were also many big guys on the field. But I thought little about it because my thoughts were mainly elsewhere. Gloria was now pregnant with our third child, Diego, who was born in April, a few weeks early. I was then in Argentina for about three months. We named him after Diego Maradona. I was at the birth, and Diego was also born by Caesarean section.

For the first few weeks everything seemed to be going well and we regularly took Diego to the hospital in Santa Fe for a check-up. But after a few weeks, his situation changed. At home I saw Diego crying – tears were running down his cheeks – but I didn't hear him. No sound came out. It was very weird, so we went to the hospital again, but they couldn't help him there. They didn't know what was wrong with him. The doctor squeezed Diego to make him cry. After all, he had to see what I meant. He knew immediately that something wasn't right and referred us to Buenos Aires, to a larger hospital. Diego and Gloria were flown in on a special plane for patient transport. Then I drove with Latifah and Khadija by car to Buenos Aires, about 500 kilometres away. In the meantime I had explained what the situation was at the club. They didn't mind me going to Buenos Aires and thought it was understandable, even though training and playing wasn't possible because of the distance. They knew the situation and supported me.

Diego ended up in the hospital in intensive care. The weeks passed and turned into a few months. All this time I rented a hotel room near the hospital. I went three or four times a day, every day, to be with Diego and help him when needed. I even flew a pastor from Ghana to Argentina to try and assist. Meanwhile, we also took care of Latifah and Khadija, of course. Diego was no longer able to swallow on his own. He was given a probe that went in through an incision in his throat so that he could be fed that way. Other than that, he seemed normal, except maybe he was a little fat. Meanwhile, the doctors had no idea what was going on. They ran all kinds of tests but they simply didn't know what was wrong with him. I asked if they would take some blood from him and some skin. I sent it to a lab in the United States for testing. Result: nothing. It did cost a lot of money with the tests, the hospital, the hotel, food, etc. After a few months I prayed to God and asked for help. What should I do? I wasn't playing football, I looked after the kids, rented a hotel room for months, and paid the expensive hospital bills. I was through with it; it all became too much for me.

A few days later I decided to go to Santa Fe, to the club. I'd already spent my earned money on all the costs we had incurred at that time so I wanted to ask for an advance so that I could pay all the bills. Before I left, I just wanted to say goodbye to Diego. I was standing next to him, and at that moment he squeezed my index finger with his little hand. He held my finger very tightly and wouldn't let go, as if he were saying, 'Don't go. Stay here.' He held my finger like this for ten minutes until the doctor decided to remove his hand. Then I got up and took the plane to Santa Fe. When I landed there and turned on my phone, I immediately got a call from Gloria. Diego had passed away. Not wanting to let go of my finger turned out to be a message from him. Diego died on 18 October.

I couldn't do much at that moment. I felt so very sad. I was there on my own and I don't think I've ever felt so lonely. Even now it's hard to talk about the pain I felt. I don't remember certain details of that moment; I only feel the pain. The next day I decided to go to the club and explain everything before flying back to Buenos Aires. That conversation was pointless. At Santa Fe I'd only signed a contract for half a season, and that was over. Because of the situation with Diego I hadn't been at the club very much, so it was too risky for them to extend my contract just like that. But when Diego died, the transfer market was also closed and I could no longer be registered. Back in Buenos Aires, the doctors in the hospital couldn't say anything new. One doctor just said that, with the knowledge he had at the time, there was indeed a chance that we could have a child who wasn't quite healthy. That's all I found out.

We buried Diego in Buenos Aires, after a church service. A few team-mates, including Pablo Bezombe, were also there. It was never the plan to bury him in Ghana; we never thought about that. That story is also online somewhere, that we weren't allowed to transfer his body to Ghana by the authorities. It's not true. We just wanted to bury Diego in Buenos Aires, where he died.

I had a lot of support from some good friends in Argentina. The people there are warm and very cordial. Also, the guys from the team, although I hadn't had much contact with them of course. They invited me to dinner. It was very nice, but to be honest I hardly know anyone from that squad of Santa Fe anymore. I played very little there because of that situation. After Diego's death, I wanted to get out of there as soon as possible. I didn't think much about it anymore. Names, places; I just don't remember. The only one I remember from then is Pablo Bezombe, a midfielder. He showed himself to be a good friend and helped me a lot. He visited the hospital a few times, and took care of me and the children. That is why I later gave Diego a second name: Diego Pablo.

When Diego passed away in Argentina, of course I also passed on the news to my family in Ghana. But I didn't hear much from them. That was partly because of my relationship with Gloria. They thought I was mostly focused on her and not paying attention to the rest of the family. I remember my brother Odartie once visiting me in England. I was playing for Aston Villa at the time and arranged for him to come to England. He wanted to work there. He also met Gloria, and that became a problem because he didn't like her. My marriage to Gloria didn't help my family. Odartie stayed in England when I left there, but at some point he had to leave the country and returned to Ghana.

I hadn't played much at Santa Fe due to the sad circumstances, so it's difficult to judge that season. I only played six games in total. It was a nice team, and a nice club too. Although it was a small club compared to Boca

Juniors, I saw it as a new beginning. My goal was to play at Boca Juniors after that, but it didn't happen. It's a shame I couldn't make that dream come true.

Because I wanted to leave Argentina, I decided to contact Anderlecht. It sounds crazy, but at that moment I thought I was still under contract with Anderlecht. I called them, but during that conversation I was told that they no longer owned me and hadn't done for a long time. I didn't know that at all. I was very surprised. I wanted to leave Argentina because of the death of my son and then I got to hear this too. I was mad at Antonio Caliendo because of me not knowing about such things at all. I called Caliendo and told him what I had been told. He got angry too, and said I didn't understand anything. It was only a brief conversation as he cut it off quickly and said he'd get back to me. Conversations with him were already quite difficult anyway because he hardly spoke English. After our phone call, he contacted a business partner of his in Argentina. He came to visit me at my hotel and wanted to explain things, wanting everything to be OK. They offered to keep paying me even though I didn't have a new club yet. They would then look for a new club for me. I said no. I wanted to get rid of Caliendo. A few days after that conversation, Caliendo himself came to Argentina. We talked about the situation.

He begged me to stay with him. Finally I said I would think about it, but it was already clear what I thought about it.

That was the last time I spoke to him. I never asked how much money he made off me, or how much money he withheld. I never got an explanation from him either. He never explained the contracts I had to sign. I had no idea about how that stuff worked. I was only concerned with football. And even if I'd read everything, I still wouldn't have understood many things from the contract. So there's no wonder I didn't realise I'd been sold a few times and not loaned out as I thought. All I had to do was sign, nothing else. But I was too trusting. I thought he treated me well and I had had no reason not to trust him. He kept in touch with me; every now and then I got something nice from him. In retrospect that was his way of gaining my trust. But maybe those gifts were paid for with my own money.

I later learned that Aston Villa had bought me in 1994 for about $1.3m. I should have received a signing-on fee there, too, but I never saw any of it. My salary did increase there but I have no idea if Caliendo withheld some of it. It was the same story at Coventry. I got paid every month, but I suspect that amount should have been much higher. After all, Caliendo had a power of attorney to arrange everything on my behalf. I don't know if he took part of my salary, but it wouldn't surprise me. In retrospect it was very naive of me not to suspect anything after he demanded the signing money back from Coventry. And I'm also sure that my transfer to Venezia was also a money issue. Somehow that was a good deal for him.

It sounds sour, but precisely because Diego died and I wanted to leave Argentina, I found out that Caliendo wasn't being honest. How different could things have turned out if Diego hadn't died? Otherwise I might have ended up working with him for longer. At that time I was paid, I played well, it was a nice country and Boca Juniors kept an eye on me. What more could I have wished for at that moment? But that's not how things ended up going.

Nii's mother
Margaret

Nii's oldest photo: at
a young age in Accra.

Nii (left) as a youngster at Kaloum
Stars in Accra.

Lamptey — the next king of world socce

as of Johan Cruyff. "Every

'ODARTEY LAMPTEY
IS THE NEW PELE'

'Nii Lamptey is the new Pelé': newspapers in 1989 and 1990

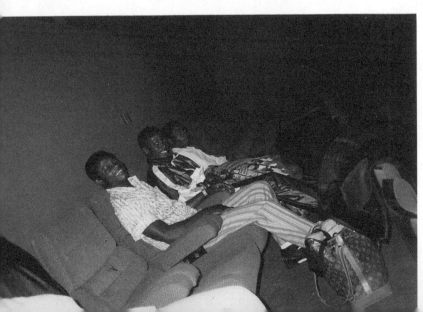

With Yaw
Preko and
Isaac Asare
in the
cinema,
1991.
Lucy van
den Borre

(Top) Sunday chickenday at the Van Den Borre family in Brussels. Lucy van den Borre

(Middle) Nii Lamptey signing autographs after a match, September 1991. Lucy van den Borre

(Bottom) Nii Lamptey at Anderlecht, October 1991

(Top) Starlets 91 Road in Accra, the street near the Accra Sports Stadium, named after the Black Starlets of 1991.
Joris Kaper

(Left) Nii and Isaac Asare dacing in the clubhouse of Anderlecht, 1992.
Lucy van den Borre

Nii playing for the national team of Ghana in the final of the Africa Cup, January 1992.

Nii playing for Ghana at the 1992 Olympics in Barcelona.

Nii playing for PSV against Ajax, September 1993.

(Top) Nii with his father Martin Lamptey and his half-brothers, 1991.

(Middle) Nii at Aston Villa, September 1994.

(Bottom) Nii at Coventry City, September 1995

Nii in the shirt of Greuther Fürth, 1999/2000.

Spielvereinigung Greuther Fürth

norisbank

(Top) The Glow Lamp Soccer Academy of Nii in Abreshia - Elmina. Joris Kaper

(Left) The Glow Lamp International School in Accra, founded by Nii. Joris Kaper

Nii as a football pundit on TV.

Nii as a coach of one of his football academy teams.

Nii coaching at one of his football academy teams.

Nii at his farm.

(Right) Nii as happy as could be with his daughters Malaika (right) and Manal.

(Bottom left) Nii with his daughters in 2019.

(Bottom right) Nii's son Mahal in a jersey of PSV, 2019.

Chapter 12

Back to Europe

AFTER ARGENTINA I decided to return to Ghana, just to recover from everything in a familiar environment. I was broken. I had spent almost all my money on the situation with Diego, I was very sad and didn't feel like playing football anymore. I stayed in Ghana for a while before returning to Europe. Friends convinced me that I had to pick myself up again. I had to start playing again, even if only to make money. And they were right. I had to try to leave everything behind. I had no choice, no matter how sad it was.

At the end of 1997 I returned to Europe and was able to try out at Auxerre in France, under coach Guy Roux. I was there for about ten days but it didn't lead to a contract. At the time, I wasn't very surprised because I hadn't played football for a few months after the drama with Diego. I was not sharp, not fit. I then came into contact with a new agent from Germany, Oliver König.

* * *

König: 'Sometime at the end of 1997 I was approached by some Ghanaian players, including Tony Yeboah, who was playing in Germany at the time for Hamburger SV. They asked if I couldn't do something for Nii Lamptey because he was without a club. I really wanted to give it a go. At that moment I saw someone who was completely struck down. Mentally, physically and financially. That's why I wanted to help him. The most obvious option was to get him to Germany. I'm from there and have good contacts there. I took him to Germany, where he first took shelter with my parents. Later we arranged a hotel for him. In Germany there was some interest from 1. FC Kaiserslautern but the transfer window was already closed, just like in the rest of Europe.

'There was really only one somewhat interesting market and that was Turkey. It wasn't the intention in advance to bring him to Turkey, but there weren't many options. But the most important thing for me was that Nii needed to get back to playing football and get his life back on track. Through an agent in Turkey, I managed to arrange for Nii to sign with Ankaragücü for half a season. In retrospect it was a pity that it didn't work out with Kaiserslautern, because they surprisingly became champions of Germany that season.'

Nii: 'Oliver was an agent for a few other Ghanaian footballers. I got on well with him; we were about the same age. So he was very young for an agent. He arranged for me to come to Ankaragücü. It was a small club in Turkey, but I didn't mind. I was happy to be able to play football again. I hadn't played football for several months; my mind was not on it. I got a six-month contract with Ankaragücü. If that suited them, they had an option to keep me longer.'

* * *

Ankaragücü's team wasn't worth a mention. But that makes sense because it was a small club. Of my team-mates there, I hung out a lot with Ohene Kennedy and Stephen Baidoo, who were also from Ghana. Kennedy now lives in London and Baidoo in Takoradi in Ghana. He also runs his own football academy there, which he named after Ankaragücü: Ankara Sporting Club of Ghana. I also got on well with Fernand Coulibaly from Mali. He was a crazy boy. He was also a good signboard for the club, a striking appearance too. He had such a great Rasta haircut.

It was difficult for us to communicate in Turkey. When we wanted to go somewhere by taxi, we always said to those drivers, 'Ankaragücü, Ankaragücü.' Then we pointed to ourselves, and they knew who we were. They would always take us everywhere for free. I also know Hasan Şaş from that team. He was known as a rising star in Turkey at the time. He didn't see me as a team-mate, but as a competitor. We both played as attacking midfielders. That's also the reason I once got into a fight with him. During a training session we had exchanged words with each other when suddenly he hit me, and I fell to the ground. Fellow players tried to calm him down, including Ohene and Stephen. I was very angry. I got up, ran after him and punched him hard. We then had to meet with the chairman of the club, and there we apologised. At the end of the season, Şaş left for Galatasaray where he tested positive for doping not much later and was banned for six months.

* * *

Oliver: 'I was surprised to hear that Nii had punched someone. He wasn't that kind of person, so something had to have happened for Nii to do something like that. It's also the only time I've experienced anything like this with him. Hasan Şaş saw Nii as an enemy from day one, which he isn't of course. That feud with Şaş actually meant the end for Nii at Ankaragücü. Şaş was the board's great talent and darling. After that fight, Nii couldn't do much good anymore according to them and so they decided not to continue with him after that season. Too bad because he actually did quite well there.'

Nii: 'Life outside of football in Turkey was quite individualistic. But the city of Ankara was nice. You could eat delicious food there, and you had a lot of jewellers there. Gloria often went shopping there, of course with my money. She regularly bought jewellery, often gold. Some other football players went out there a lot. To nightclubs, for example, that sort of thing. That wasn't my thing, so in Turkey I often stayed in my own house. Always with football on TV.'

* * *

That half a season at Ankaragücü actually went pretty well. We finished 13th in the league but the differences were small. Three more points and we would have finished eighth; three points fewer and we were relegated. We won that season against the Fenerbahçe, who had Jay-Jay Okacha, and Beşiktaş, who had Daniel Amokachi. I played ten games and finally scored again. But because of that argument with Hasan Şaş, I had no choice but to leave that summer.

I then came into contact with Vanio Kostov, an agent from Bulgaria. He had previously played in Portugal, which was why he had many contacts there. He was the agent for several other Ghanaian players at the time, three of whom played for União Leiria. I suspect that I came into contact with Kostov through them. He made sure I could join União Leiria, and I signed a one-year contract with an option to extend. União Leiria was also a small club but with a wealthy owner, João Bartolomeu.

It wouldn't have mattered much if the transfer hadn't gone through. One other agent saw his chance to defame me at that club. It was Domenico Ricci. That Italian wanted to become my agent years earlier, but I chose Antonio Caliendo at the time. Apparently he was still mad about that. He now saw his chance to defame me at the club, so that deal almost fell through. He later delivered similar tricks to a few other football players from Ghana. They really wished Ricci dead.

Emmanuel Duah, Maxwell Konadu and Augustine Ahinful also played for Leiria. With that I became the fourth Ghanaian in the squad. It made my early days there a bit easier. I've known them for a while too. Duah was also on the Ghana under-16 squad when we won the World Cup in 1991, scoring the winning goal in the final. Maxwell Konadu was with me in the during the Olympic Games in 1992, and Augustine Ahinful was also in the squad for the U-20 World Cup. Augustine left after a few months on loan to my old club Venezia. I also remember Paulo Duarte from the squad. He married the daughter of the chairman and later became national coach of Burkina Faso and Gabon. Fernando Baptista was a nice goalkeeper and Habib Sissoko was also a good player. Ricardo Silva was a crazy one with a good shot. João Manuel Loureiro dos Santos passed away in 2005 from multiple sclerosis.

Gloria, Latifah and Khadija were also with me in Portugal and Turkey. I heard some rumours around that time that Gloria was sleeping with other men because I wouldn't have time for her or wouldn't make time for her, and that I went to other countries on my own to play football, leaving her behind with the children. But that wasn't true. Gloria went with me to every country I played in, except later to China. The kids loved it everywhere, and that was lucky. But they were also very young. I wanted to give them a good education because I know what I missed in the past myself. That's why, when they had to go to school, they went to an international private school in every country where we lived. I've spent a lot of money on them for education.

During my stay in Portugal something strange happened. At one point I had a problem with a wisdom tooth, so I went to a dentist who told me to have that tooth extracted. I wondered why because it didn't bother me that much. But it turned out that they accidentally mixed up the X-ray pictures of my teeth with someone else's. So my wisdom tooth was pulled, but it didn't have to come out at all! I was angry for a while and a few people said I should sue them. But in the end I didn't. I just let it be; I didn't feel like the hassle at all. Emmanuel and Maxwell thought it was hilarious; they bullied me a lot in the months that followed! In the end I was able to laugh about it myself.

The season at União Leiria went very well for the club. We finished sixth and were one point short of European football but, despite missing out, it was a very good outcome as Leiria had only been promoted to the top division the previous season. And the stadium was always quite full for a small club. Unfortunately I didn't get to play much myself and only appeared in seven games. I actually have no idea how that came about, but apparently our coach Mário Reis didn't see enough potential in me.

Because I played little, I wanted to leave after that season. I then again contacted Oliver König, who had helped me get a contract with Ankaragücü a season earlier. It seemed a good idea to Oliver that I would go back to Germany because I was at a dead end in Portugal. He was able to guide me well there and so I decided to leave for Germany.

Chapter 13

Restart in Germany

OLIVER KÖNIG: 'After the season at União Leiria, Nii contacted me again. I was then able to arrange a contract with SpVgg Greuther Fürth, who played in the 2. Bundesliga. It was a small club so maybe it wasn't the best choice. But at the time there weren't many options. We therefore talked to clubs with whom we had good contacts. The conversation at Greuther Fürth was positive, but there were still some doubts with the coach, Benno Möhlmann. He wondered how someone like Nii Lamptey could end up at a small club like Greuther Fürth. However, the chairman thought it was all right and managed to convince Möhlmann. Nii was given a contract for one season, but soon his contract was extended for another year during the season.'

Nii: 'I was a free transfer, so I didn't cost the club a fee. Greuther Fürth had ambition, good facilities and German football was highly regarded, so I was also interested in a transfer to Germany even though the club played at the second level. I was well received at the club; everything was well arranged. Of the players, I still remember Rachid Azzouzi, a Moroccan midfielder. I liked him very much. And I also know Faouzi Rouissi from Tunisia, and Oliver Schmidt, a defender. I also remember Frank Turr. He was always very quiet, but he would go on a rampage on the field.

'The atmosphere at the club wasn't comparable to Argentina, for example. It was a lot less social. In Argentina I was immediately included in the team, I was really treated as if I was one of them. When the problems with Diego started there, they all sympathised with me. Pablo Bezombe often called, invited me over for dinner, that sort of thing. You ate together, you talked a lot. In Germany it was different. But you learn, you grow, you see that not everyone treats you the same. You have to learn to deal with that and I did that in Germany.'

* * *

In Germany I got back to playing regularly, especially in my first season. I was used a lot as a pinch hitter, especially when we were behind. Sometimes very physical football was played, which was to my disadvantage. I wasn't really tall enough. From a football point of view I think I was better than most of the other players on the team, but there was more to it because to be honest I wasn't the fittest player there was at the time. I regularly had problems with my knee, so it also made sense that I didn't play all the time.

I lived very well in Fürth. But when Fürth comes up, people are right about racism. If I were to believe all the stories online it was nothing but racism there. But that wasn't the case, although I did experience it. It's mostly small things that I noticed that sometimes haunted me. For example, when I sat down somewhere, people who sat next to me would regularly get up, or people close to me then moved to another place. Sometimes I also had that feeling on the field, that some team-mates didn't pass you the ball. Even when I entered the locker room, and I said 'good morning', sometimes hardly anyone said anything back. But when a German came in later, everyone said something back. Even though things like that don't mean anything, it was more of a feeling. It probably didn't mean anything, because with most of the team-mates I had no problems at all.

I sometimes heard curses from the German stands, although that was not always the case. I hardly ever experienced that in Belgium and the Netherlands. I only remember a match in Belgium against Ghent. I scored against them and ran to the Ghent supporters. I didn't do that on purpose. I was very happy and didn't look well enough, and thought they were Anderlecht fans. They then threw a few bananas my way. I grabbed a banana, peeled it: and took a bite!

However, there is one incident in Germany that caused a stir in the media. It's precisely that incident that painted the picture of it being all racism in that period. We often went to a training camp for matches, and at one I found myself in a room with a team-mate who didn't want that. He was one of the few players who had, shall we say, a rather right-wing political leaning. He refused to sleep in a hotel room with me.

* * *

Oliver: 'The racism story is indeed quite exaggerated because of that one incident. At the time I complained to the club about the player in question because I was very angry. That player came from the east of Germany, from a region where there were quite right-wing views. But then the incident was over again. A few years later, however, I talked about Nii's period in Germany in a documentary. And that incident also came up then. That then took on a life of its own and was greatly blown up. This created the impression that Nii was confronted with racism everywhere. In reality, that was not the case at all.'

Nii: 'I sometimes talked about racism and alleged racism with team-mate Henry Onwuzuruike. He was from Nigeria. He was crazy! He sometimes had the same feeling in the locker room. He would then walk in, say "good morning", to which he got no response. He would look around and say, "Fuck all of you"! We often just had to laugh about it. I didn't worry about it. The reason I came to Europe hadn't changed in all those years: to play football. Everything around that was much less important to me. But that's not to say that some things didn't bother me. If a team-mate doesn't want to sleep in a room with you, it hurts.

In my first season at Fürth I played 22 games and scored four times. And I played three more cup matches, in which I scored once. Sometime in my second season, however, Möhlmann was succeeded by Uwe Erkenbrecher as coach. Under him I got to play a lot less. In that season I scored once in 14 league matches and two cup matches. In that season I was in a game about to shoot when a defender arrived. We hit the ball at the same time, and then pain shot into my knee. I knew immediately that it was bad news again. I had keyhole surgery, where they told me that my knee was no longer good. The only reason I could still play football, albeit with a lot of effort, was that the muscles around that knee were very strong. Those muscles held everything together. Otherwise, it would have been the end of the story long ago.'

Oliver: 'The doctor told me that his knee was no longer good. In fact, he said it looked like a bomb had exploded in his knee. Other footballers would have stopped long ago, the knee was that bad. But the muscles around Nii's knee were extremely strong. This allowed him to continue playing. But that doctor doubted whether he could still play in, for example, the Bundesliga. At that time, a club from China happened to be interested: Shandong Luneng from Jinan. The level in China was a lot lower, but financially it was a great offer. With the news of Nii's knee in mind, I advised Nii to consider that offer.'

Nii: 'Shandong Luneng's offer came at a time when I had less and less playing time in Fürth. In addition, it was financially very interesting, so we decided to talk to that club. Coincidentally, my old Ghana under-17 coach, Otto Pfister, had also contacted me a few weeks before. He was then a trainer of Al-Zamalek in Egypt. Otto was a German, so he visited Germany regularly. During a lunch, Otto told me that he would like me to play at Al-Zamalek. But a few weeks later, that offer came from China. What I heard and saw about China, and the money involved; I then called Otto to say that I had a preference for China. He advised against that, of course. But he had his own interests because he wanted me to come to Egypt.

'Oliver then went to talk to Shandong Luneng in China. I was very curious. I liked what Oliver told me afterwards, so we decided to take the offer. Greuther Fürth also agreed to a transfer. It was a new challenge for me after two seasons in Germany. And given the situation and the money, I had to go. But it was a good choice, because I had a great time there.'

Oliver: 'It was the best solution for Nii to go to China, not only because of the money and his knee, but also for our relationship. At Fürth he made a new start, but at a club of the second level. Of course, that also meant that the contract offered a bit less financially, although Fürth didn't pay badly for a second-tier club. It was less than Nii was used to, but he was content with it. I think it was mostly a shock for Gloria.

'I discussed all the details about contracts with Nii, so as not to get any misunderstandings. Everything was clear to Nii, he said so. But after one season he started to ask some questions about certain things in his contract, things that we had discussed many times. He asked if we could change certain things in his contract, and if I could arrange that with the board. But that wasn't possible because everything had already been contractually agreed. Nii said he didn't understand some things at the time, but I explained everything in detail a few times. We had a big disagreement about that. I could not and did not want to ask the chairman to change certain financial things in the contract. We had heated discussions about that.

'But I knew the idea didn't come from him. I just knew Gloria was behind it. She saw herself as a glamour girl. She always wanted to buy expensive brands; Louis Vuitton, Gucci, that sort of thing. So I was mostly mad at her. She played Nii in a cunning way. She also knew what was in the contract. She was educated. That situation led to disagreements, and it wasn't worth it to me. That would ruin our relationship. That was the first reason to look around for a new club where he could earn more. Staying with Fürth was therefore not really an option, because then I wouldn't be able to work well with him anymore. In the end it became China, where I arranged a nice contract for him. My relationship with Nii therefore remained good, unlike my relationship with Gloria.'

Chapter 14

Happy in China

WHEN I arrived in Jinan in the summer of 2001, I immediately found the city a very pleasant place. I liked what I saw of the stadium and facilities. It was a football country on the rise. In Asia, Japan and Korea were way ahead of China, but you could tell by everything that China was also making progress. At that time more and more foreign players were recruited, but there was a maximum of four foreign players per squad. And I made good money in China, so I was happy to be there.

Gloria and the children stayed behind in Germany. Gloria was pregnant with our fourth child at the time, and the medical care in Germany was very good. In addition, in Jinan, not much English teaching was available for children, so we thought it would be better if they stayed in Germany. Shandong Luneng is the only club to which Gloria and the kids didn't move with me. We decided that they would live in Germany for a while, until after the birth of our fourth child. After that they would return to Ghana, also considering the education of Latifah and Khadija. We wanted to send them to a Ghanaian school at a certain age.

At the switch to Shandong Luneng, the league season was halfway through. Boris Ignatyev, a Russian, was the coach. I remember Li Go Zhu from the team, and Li Xiaopeng. He was a good player. Li Go Zhu was a friend there, he was crazy! He always took me everywhere; he liked that. And he tried to teach me Chinese. Of course, he taught me all the Chinese swear words first! I can still say them. We were both very sober too. Practically everyone there was. The Chinese don't like it when someone steps out of line thinking they're better than the rest. That mentality and atmosphere suited me well. I'm also modest and don't have a big mouth.

There was also a Russian on the team, Sergey Kiryakov. He thought he was the star player, and he behaved like one. That's why many players didn't like him. They didn't even want to talk to him. But he was lucky that we also had a Russian coach. Communicating in China was otherwise very difficult. It was a completely different language and alphabet, and extremely difficult. The moment I signed there I was immediately assigned an interpreter. All communication went through him, and he went almost everywhere with me. Luckily I got by without an interpreter on the football field, which was often no problem.

The fans were also happy with me, sometimes chanting my name. When I went into town and I wanted to buy something, they often wouldn't even take my money. I'd get something for free, or at least a big discount. Although Jinan was a big city, I was the only black player on our team and you didn't see many black people there, so I was also quickly noticed on the street. Then complete strangers would come up to me and wanted to touch my skin! They were very curious. Most would just look at me for a moment, but some were a bit bolder, and they'd feel on my skin. But it didn't mean anything, it wasn't racist. They weren't used to it and were just curious.

Gloria finally gave birth to a daughter in the hospital in late September 2001. We named her Lisa. Her birth was a success. I wasn't present because I was in China at the time, but the club gave me permission to travel directly to Germany. But after a few weeks it became clear that something was wrong with Lisa too. She could barely breathe on her own. She was then taken to the intensive care unit where she spent several months. Lisa also received a probe through her nose, but nothing could be done for her either. I felt so incredibly powerless. Just like with Diego, I also had a pastor from Ghana come over for Lisa. I paid for a ticket for him so he could pray for her survival.

However, I couldn't stay long in Germany at that time. My career had suffered greatly while Diego was in hospital. I then stopped playing football to take care of him, and because of that I lost a lot. I couldn't risk that again. So at some point I decided to return to China so that I could make some money to pay for Lisa's care. If it were possible, I'd fly back to Germany to visit Lisa, and of course I was in frequent contact with Gloria. That went on for several months. It was difficult, but I had no choice. I got through it all right.

In December 2001 the season ended, and we had finished sixth. I'd played 18 of the 26 league games and scored five goals. I felt good and was in the right place there. It even went so well that the then national team coach, Fred Osam-Duodu, tried to convince me sometime in 2001 to play for Ghana again. I remembered him as the coach of Ghana under-20s, with whom we won the African Championship in 1993 and lost the World Cup Final later that year. My relationship with him was good. That was also the reason for me to reconsider my decision not to play for the Ghana national team anymore. Moreover, Abédi

Pelé, who didn't want to play in the same team with me, had ended his career.

Fred persuaded me to make myself available to the Black Stars again. I got permission from Shandong Luneng to travel to Ghana, but the international match in question was cancelled. I was already at the airport in China when I heard the news. I went back home and after that nothing changed regarding the postponement. Osam-Duodu sadly passed away in 2016 after a short illness.

Ignatyev, then still a coach at Shandong Luneng, didn't like my possible return to Ghana at all. He was even angry and wondered why I should go to the national team again. He wanted me to stay in China and even said I didn't deserve to go at all. I was quite angry about that so, in the next game, against Beijing Guoan, I wanted to prove something. I was annoyed and scored twice; we won 2-0. I played really well and after that second goal I walked over to him. I took the shirt I was wearing and said to him, 'Yes, I deserve to play in the Ghana shirt.' After the game he apologised to me. That had to be done according to someone from the board. That settled things for me a bit.

Ignatyev and I weren't really into each other, and I can't really explain why. It happened a few times that I was better with the board of a club than with the coach.

That was somewhat the case with Ignatyev, but also with Valeri Nepomniachi. He succeeded Ignatyev in December 2001, after the season ended. Nepomniachi also came from Russia. Despite that change I continued to play regularly, and my time there went really well. In my second season with Shandong Luneng we came fourth. I played 19 out of 30 games and scored twice. But I didn't click with Nepomniachi, who was very critical of me.

It was sometime in early June 2002 when Gloria called me. I was at my house in Jinan at the time. She told me Lisa had passed away. Unfortunately, what I had been expecting for a long time had happened. Of course I was sad, but somehow I knew it was inevitable, with Diego's situation in mind. The next morning I went to the club and told my coach what had happened. I then had a meeting with the chairman and management and told them the same thing. They were very sorry for what had happened, and they gave me a week off to go to Germany and arrange Lisa's funeral. They then also gave a small amount of money to help with the expenses I had incurred. It was a nice gesture from them. Naturally, the conversations all went through my interpreter.

Lisa had exactly the same problem as Diego, and the doctors couldn't help her either. Even now there is nothing concrete I can say about what Diego and Lisa died from. When Diego and Lisa were alive, I sent some of their blood and skin to labs in Germany and the United States. That also made me little wiser, except learning that it was something genetic. It turned out that there was a chance that our children would have an abnormality. All I can say is that they could barely breathe on their own. Lisa and Diego were also physically unwell. You saw it in the way they looked, in their faces and in the way they lay sometimes. We buried Lisa in Fürth. First there was a meeting at church, where we prayed for her. Some friends were there, people who had helped us and some former team-mates. Then we went to the cemetery where we buried Lisa. I hope no one has to go through this too. Both were very sad and unpleasant experiences. Fortunately, God has given me the strength to get through this pain.

During that period I had also bought a house in Accra, because it was intended that Gloria and the children would return to Ghana after Lisa was born. That's why I bought a lot of stuff in Germany. A couple of couches, a freezer, that sort of thing. We had all of that shipped to Ghana so we were also busy arranging everything for that move, which was extremely hectic. Fortunately there was another family in Germany, the Ruth family, who helped us to arrange everything there, which was very nice. They helped us organise the funeral and often visited Lisa's grave. Later they even visited Ghana. They were supporters of Fürth. Unfortunately, contact with them has since dwindled.

After Lisa's funeral it was very difficult when I had to go back to China. I went back on my own and was very sad. I kept crying on the way. I was alone; Gloria and the children stayed behind in Germany. Shortly afterwards they returned to Ghana. I had a very hard time, but when I returned to Jinan I also had to do my job again. And that was equally important to me. Don't get me wrong, family is very important – it is the key to success. But without my job I couldn't support my family. Whatever the situation was at the time, I also wanted to play football again. That was my first priority. Everything else I just tried to forget.

* * *

Nii: 'Besides playing football in China, I also tried to help Gloria in Ghana to set up my own company. She came to visit me in China at one point and was impressed by those typical Chinese lanterns. We decided to buy a quantity of them and ship them to Ghana so she could sell them there. We also bought a lot of children's black shoes. Children in Ghana are obliged to wear these to school, in combination with white socks. The intention was that Gloria could then sell them in Ghana. Result: zero. Nothing. I put $5,000 into it, but she didn't do anything with it. I knew that both products would sell well in Ghana and that she could make money with them, but Gloria didn't do anything with it. She made no effort at all. Those lanterns and shoes were collecting dust in the garage of our house. It was wasted money.'

Oliver: 'In the last months of 2002 Nii played a little less. Nepomniachi clearly wanted to get rid of Nii in my eyes. At that time there was a rule that a maximum of three or four foreigners could be in a squad. Nepomniachi wanted to bring his own players to the club, or players from agent friends, probably because he could earn something from doing this. To make room for that, he tried to bully Nii away. Incomprehensible, because Nii played well in China and was extremely popular. Even to this day they still know him at the club, despite the fact that many other famous footballers are heading that way these days. But Nepomniachi managed to finish fourth with the club that season, a good result. He was therefore given the benefit of the doubt and Nii's expiring contract was not renewed. I thought he was abusing his position as a coach.'

Nii: 'What I did dislike about China was travelling over there. That took a lot of time. The away games, we always went by plane. I wasn't a fan of that, I always found it scary. I hate flying. Having to travel to all the away games by plane was no fun. I'm always scared when I have to fly, but I always would go. I didn't miss a single game because of that fear. I didn't have much choice, did I? In September 2001 you also had those attacks in the United States with those planes; that didn't really help either. I was flying in a plane back to Ghana, or to China, I don't remember. I had a long layover somewhere. I therefore spent the night in a hotel because I didn't fly on until the next morning. I turned on the television in my hotel room and then saw the images of those attacks. Man, was I scared! All that flying to those away games was definitely the least fun thing in China. But, all in all, my time in China was very nice. The period when Lisa died and the aftermath of course not, but otherwise I had a very good time. I fell in love with that country and the people, and the people there fell in love with me too. They nicknamed me "Little Diamond" there.'

Chapter 15

Start of my school

WHILE WAITING for a new club, I decided to return to Ghana where I stayed for a few months. During my time in China I'd bought that house in Accra where Gloria and the children were going to live. I wanted to work on that, and besides, it was nice to be with my family again after a long time. I wasn't afraid that my career was over because Oliver König was looking for a new club for me in the meantime. At that time, we were mainly looking for a club where I could earn good money because I didn't know how my knee would be. And, of course, I'd lost a lot of money in my career looking after Diego and Lisa, plus probably the money that went into Antonio Caliendo's pockets.

Such a club was of course not immediately to be found. We first looked for a new club in China, but there was the SARS outbreak in late 2002 and early 2003. As a result the rules for travelling to China from Ghana at the time were quite strict and difficult. Oliver therefore started looking outside of China. A few months later I was at home when Oliver contacted me. He told me that a club from Dubai was interested. I knew in advance that the level was not that high, but I must say that the offer was financially very attractive. There was no doubt that I would take this offer.

* * *

Oliver: 'At that time I was doing a lot of business in Dubai where I'd met the club owner of Al-Nasr, among others. He was looking for a certain type of player and I suggested Nii. I didn't really expect anything to come from that, because when I started talking about Nii, I didn't think he took me seriously. But then an offer came out of nowhere. Al-Nasr was interested in a transfer from Nii because of his name. But they wanted to know if he could still do it. In the summer of 2003, they had a training camp in France where Nii joined and played a match. They were happy with the result, so they decided to commit Nii for a year. Nii got a lot of contract money, in addition to his monthly salary. I was a little concerned about the medical examination because of Nii's knee. So, when Al-Nasr's club doctor got to his knee, I started distracting him a bit so that he wouldn't give his full attention to that knee. Nii passed the inspection.'

Nii: 'When I arrived in Dubai, the club gave me a car. A Ford, including a driver. I wasn't allowed to drive there yet; in Dubai you had to get a separate driver's licence. A driver's licence from another country wasn't valid there. Later, I got my licence. Then I could drive myself. One of the first things I wanted to do when I got there was shop in one of the malls. The cars I saw – there isn't a single expensive car brand that wasn't there. Lamborghini, Ferrari; I looked at them open-mouthed! "What is this? Where did I end up?" I wondered. It's not a place for football. If you're planning to retire from football, you should cash in there. That's the only logical reason. But when I started playing there, I had the idea that I wasn't done with football yet. That I could still do it, even though I hadn't played for half a year.'

* * *

I quite enjoyed it in Dubai, but it was very difficult to play there. Those club owners are so incredibly rich, football is just a game to them; it's just for fun. Playing as a close-knit team was also not an option. I was supposed to pass to fellow players, but don't think I ever got the ball back. Some players were even able to blame someone else if they missed an opportunity themselves. And, meanwhile, they expected me to dribble across the entire pitch and then score. They didn't understand football; it was really not to be taken seriously. I really don't know the names of all those Al-Nasr players anymore. All kinds of names like Khalifa and Sheik! I even forgot who our coach was – all I know is that he was from abroad.

Before the league started in Dubai, the President's Cup – the cup tournament of the United Arab Emirates – took place. That tournament was played in the first round in a competition format with four groups of seven clubs, with the top four clubs from each group going through to the next stage. From that round it was a play-off system. However, with Al-Nasr we were out in that next round. The first round took a very long time, longer even than the league, which consisted of only ten games. But the league also did not go well. In our group with six clubs we finished fourth; Al-Nasr lost in the play-off match for seventh place, meaning we finished eighth in the league. At that moment I think I'd already left Al-Nasr. Sometime in October I injured my knee again. I then went to London for keyhole surgery, and I stayed there for about three weeks. They didn't tell me much about my knee. Since my period at Aston Villa I had regularly suffered from it, and before I started again at Al-Nasr I had of course not played for half a year. So it wasn't so strange that I felt that knee a lot.

That was also the reason why I didn't play much at Al-Nasr. But that was expected of me, especially as a foreigner. It just wasn't possible at the time. Since the club was only allowed to have three or four foreigners under contract, they decided to buy off my contract so that they could sign someone else. I ended up leaving just before the end of the season. Still, I played at Al-Nasr for a total of about eight months. And I made good money there! But because I started getting more and more problems with that knee, I slowly started to realise that the end of my career was in sight. I noticed that because of that knee I was no longer as fast as before. Slowly but surely I started to think more and more about my life after football.

* * *

Oliver: 'At that moment I thought that knee wouldn't last much longer. I thought it was pointless to continue playing football any longer. I was already surprised that Nii had passed the medical tests in China and Dubai. Nii didn't play much at the end of the season with Al-Nasr because of that knee. After the club ended his contract, I told Nii it had been nice. He had earned well in China and Dubai. He was able to say goodbye to his football career with honour.'

Nii: 'The very first time I started thinking about life after my football career was when I was still playing in

China. I knew someone who was setting up a hospital in Accra. But he ran into financial problems and had to sell the land where he wanted to build the hospital. The foundation for the hospital was already there, but construction had been halted. That man contacted me and asked if I might be interested in the soil. He came to me because I'd already bought a large plot of land elsewhere in Accra, in the East Legon neighbourhood. I had my house built there. He thought that maybe that's why I might be interested in this piece of land. And I was, but I wanted to wait on that until I was back in Ghana. After my period in China, I stayed in Ghana for a few months, and I visited the plot of land. At that time there was nothing else, no houses or anything. Only an empty space, with the foundation of the hospital on it. At that moment I decided that I wanted to start a school there.'

* * *

In the end we came to an agreement, and I bought the land. I adapted the building plans so that the building eventually became a school and not a hospital. When construction was underway, and it was announced that I was going to start a school, people came to congratulate me. They thought it was a great idea and wondered how I had come up with it. The reactions were very positive. That gave me even more energy to really make something of it. And that was nice because I actually knew nothing about that business. However, those reactions made me determined to keep going, even though I didn't know what to expect in the future. Education, of course, had been a problem for me in my youth and because of that I had a lot of difficulties, and also at a later age when I became a professional football player. The contracts and documents I signed? No idea what was in them. I lost a lot of money because of this. That's why I set up that school, so that at least other children wouldn't suffer the way I did. That's the best thing you can give your child these days: a good education.

I started small, very small even. In 2004 I opened the school. I called it the Glow Lamp International School. I read somewhere about the expression 'light in the dark'. I liked that. A person who walks in the dark needs light to see. The light shows you the way. I thought of that. It's inspiring; that's what attracted me. So, it's really a coincidence that 'Glow' and 'Lamp' seem to be the abbreviations of Gloria and Lamptey. I started the school with just one student. She was only three years old, still very young. But she did come to school every morning. I should really thank her father. He brought her to the school; he had faith in it. I was the director of the school and I had hired a teacher especially for her. She was of course happy when more students came to the school after a few months. Then the second year started, and the number of students rose to 18. Then I also started promoting the school.

When the school opened, it was still under construction. The ground floor was usable but the second and third floors were not finished. They were still being worked on. So I did take the future of the school into account. I took it seriously. The entire building was completed within a year and, in the years that followed, the school really started to grow. The number of students is now fairly stable at around 400 every year. As the school grew, I naturally had to hire more staff. I still do that all myself now. I review the applicants' letters and, based on that, I schedule a few interviews with candidates that seem the best to me. I know what kind of person I am looking for and how much salary they can earn.

In the years that followed, when the number of students started to increase, I hired buses to pick up the children at home and take them back. But that was easier said than done; many drivers were not honest. They would sometimes stop somewhere at random, and then tell the children to walk on because the road had been broken open or that the bus had a flat tyre or breakdown. But that was nonsense. They just did it to save money and time. Some of them even made deals at petrol stations. They'd fill up with petrol for a certain amount, but the receipt would state a much higher cost, and then they would declare that figure to me. When I found out, I stopped doing that. I now have two buses left and four I rent from a company. I only pay for those if everything goes well – when all children have been picked up and taken home in the afternoon.

At the school we now also have a dedicated class for autistic students. Most schools in Ghana don't have that, although I don't think it's very special either. I wanted to do that because I was thinking about Diego and Lisa. I thought about them when they were in the hospital and their situation. If they had survived, I knew they would need special education. That's why I wanted something like this in my school. And from the beginning I had the idea for a day care, which I started a few years after the start of the school. So, it's not only a school, but also a nursery. Because the building was still under construction, that wasn't desirable at the beginning with all that noise.

I named all the classrooms after the countries where I played football. I have memories of every country. Strangely enough they are mostly good memories because I mainly think about the positives. And I wanted to have something tangible of my career close to me. The names are not only from club level, but also countries where I played with Ghana and have nice memories of, such as Switzerland, Mexico and Brazil. I mentioned them in the same order as my career path. So the first locale is of course called Belgium.

The students who've graduated from my school generally end up doing well. They work or continue their studies. Some are even in parliament! For me that's very nice – to give them something I didn't have myself.

When I went abroad again in the summer of 2003 to play football in Dubai, I was actually afraid to go. I was busy building my school at the time. But I was also busy setting up another company. I invested a lot of money there but I knew that Gloria was not the right person to keep an eye on that company during my absence. She just didn't have that knowledge and skill. I had helped her set up a business three times over the years, but she didn't do anything with them. And so she didn't make any money either. That was the case with those lanterns and shoes from China, but also when I played in Portugal. Then I'd set up a wine shop for her. That didn't work at all, it was a disaster. She had an education and went to school but she just didn't do anything with it. I didn't understand that. Am I not able to run a school for years without going to school much myself?

196

That company I'd started was a distribution centre for products from Nestlé, among others. It was the largest distribution centre of the Ghanaian region of Kasoa. I put in $10,000 myself. I had appointed a few people but they eventually messed it all up. They destroyed that company. The person who introduced me to that business said that if I wanted to quit, I would get my $10,000 back too. He said the investment could be worth $15,000 after six months. It seemed like a good investment and it started well. But when I left for Dubai I had little insight into it and had to trust the people I had appointed. When I returned to Ghana after a few months there was an audit to see if all processes in the distribution centre were going well. I took the Nestlé people there that morning, but it turned out to be a mess. I immediately decided to stop with it. The Nestlé people wanted me to continue but I told them I couldn't. I couldn't be there often at that time and therefore had little oversight on everything, so I cancelled the lease on the space I rented, sold the van I bought for the company, and called it quits.

The moment my school started running, a few problems arose there as well. When I bought the land and started building the school, everything was fine, and the government wasn't involved. But once the school was up and running the government suddenly showed an interest and they started talking about taxes, social insurance, that sort of thing. There were all kinds of things that I knew nothing about and only then came into contact with. At one point I had to pay tax on the land I had bought myself. I get it, but it was still very frustrating. I didn't pay that tax at the beginning because it was all new to me. When I bought that piece of land, there was no government help at all. Then I built a school there, helping children to get a better education, and then the government started talking about all kinds of taxes.

A few times the government wanted to close the school, but it's a private school, so parents pay to get a good education for their children. But they sometimes wouldn't pay while their child was already at school. Because I didn't get all my money on time, sometimes I couldn't pay certain taxes on time. That is of course very difficult. But I don't think it's fair to come by and say you want to close my school without the government helping me set up, while they actually benefit from it. After all, it makes them money. But if the parents don't pay, well, I really must pay my staff's salary first. These are all challenges that come with running a school in Ghana. And I hadn't counted on them. I actually had the idea to also start a university, but because of all that government meddling I cancelled those plans.

Chapter 16

End of my career

AFTER I had returned from Dubai and had been in Ghana for almost a year, Asante Kotoko suddenly appeared on my path in June 2005, one of the top clubs in Ghana. Alhaji Salifu Abubakar, who had given me shelter when I had to leave my father's place in Kumasi, had risen to the position of interim manager there and, when he heard that I had returned to Ghana, he contacted me again. He made me an offer to come and play for Kotoko. Somehow it was a little strange because our contact had dwindled after my marriage to Gloria. But I was fine with it. I got along just fine with him at the time, albeit on a professional level. A connection like the old days, when I considered him a father, was no longer there.

* * *

Oliver König: 'After Nii's time in Dubai, I thought his career was over; also because he had started his school. But a few months later he started talking about Asante Kotoko, the most popular and biggest club in the country. They had made him an offer. I said I thought that was a bad idea because he couldn't play at 100 per cent performance anymore because of that knee. But he really wanted to do it, so it was his own decision. He didn't do it for the money and the challenge. He just wanted it.'

Nii: 'Before I left for Europe as a little boy, I'd never played in the Ghanaian Premier League. At Cornerstones I'd only played football in the second team, a youth team. And after Cornerstones my adventure in Europe began. Somehow it felt a bit like a loss. I wanted to have the Ghanaian Premier League on my CV despite the fact that the facilities here are much worse than in Europe.

'This was also a challenge; it took some getting used to when you're used to the fields in Europe. In addition, it was also something I wanted to do for the people in Kumasi. When I lived in Kumasi as a little boy, several people helped me there, including Salifu. They were fans of Kotoko and Salifu was now even in the management of the club, so I also wanted to give something back to them. It seemed like a win-win situation to me. I could continue to play football, and at the same time be involved in running my school. If you're not there yourself, then you have no idea what's happening. Unfortunately, it happens too often in Ghana that a company collapses due to poor management. And, of course, I already had that bad experience with that distribution centre. So, this was a good combination. However, it was a lot of travel. I trained and played football in Kumasi, while I lived in Accra and was also busy with my school there.'

* * *

When I decided to sign with Kotoko, I suspected it would be my last season. I hadn't played football in a while, and I was busy with my school. But still I wanted to try. After that, going abroad again was in any case out of the question. I'm not sure if I was the first Ghanaian footballer to come back from Europe to play in Ghana again, but I was the first by name. At the time the assumption in Ghana was that players returning had become a failure abroad because it was thought that they could no longer find a club in Europe.

It was not just football players either. There are plenty of examples of Ghanaians who go abroad and have to live in poverty, but when they return they pretend they've made it, while the reality is different, purely because otherwise in Ghana they're seen as a failure. It's good that players come back to Ghana after a career elsewhere and share their experiences with players here. They can learn from that experience. Look at a country like Brazil. Those who have played football in Europe very often return to Brazil at the end of their career, to finish there. The fans are thrilled with that. Here it's different. People yell after you, curse you. It's horrible. I experienced it myself in my season at Kotoko. That was sometimes difficult, especially in away games. The crowd yells at you, insults you; anything to make you play worse.

At one point I didn't feel like explaining again and again why I was playing in Ghana. I wasn't broke, I had money, so I wasn't doing it for that. Kotoko gave me a cheque for about $4,000 when I went to play there, but it turned out not to be backed. I just let it go then. I did let the club know, but never asked about the money again. They have often said they would still give it, but I never received anything. So I didn't do it for the money.

At Kotoko, there was respect for me among the younger players. They knew what I'd done in my career. Much value is placed on the opinion of an older person in Ghana. Where I could, I tried to help the younger players. I talked to them, advised them and coached them. Sometimes the salary was paid late, and sometimes not at all. I gave those players a little money. That was the rule rather than the exception. They just needed money, plain and simple. I'd help them with that and give them some. No loan or anything, they didn't have to pay it back. But I never felt like players were trying to take advantage of that. It seems like a football academy would be a logical next step after my career. But I didn't even think about that at the time.

The league in Ghana had already started in April, so I missed that because I joined in June. I soon noticed that it was sometimes quite rough. Attackers in particular suffered from this, and so did I. But most of all I had regular pain in my knee. I'd also only signed a contract for one season, so at the end of it I knew it was done. It had been beautiful. I was happy that I could at least still play for Kotoko in Ghana.

In addition, I ended my career with awards. On 1 July 2005 we won the President's Cup, which was also my first match for Kotoko. That is the anniversary of the date that Ghana became a republic under president Kwame Nkrumah, so it's kind of a tribute. We won that game 1-0 against our biggest rival, Hearts of Oak. After the President's Cup we also won the Special Cup at the beginning of September by beating Cape Coast Dwarfs over two legs. We won the first game 1-0, then away we won 2-1 and I scored the winning goal five minutes before the end. But the most important thing was of course the league, which lasted until mid-November, and in the penultimate game we were able to become champions, away at Real Tamale United. But about ten minutes before the end, when it was 0-0, that match was stopped because angry supporters of theirs came on to the field. They were angry with the referee, who had to flee to the changing rooms. We did the same and the match was of course stopped. We were escorted out of the stadium after dark as Tamale fans tried to block the roads with burning tyres.

The following week the last round of games was on the programme and because the football association had not yet made a statement about the cancelled match, we had to err on the side of caution and try to win our last fixture. In the end we won 1-0 and we were officially champions of Ghana! That abandoned game was later converted to a regular 3-0 victory. We were presented with the trophy after our last game, a great moment. I was already very happy to be able to play for Kotoko, but to also become champion was wonderful.

The start of the following season, 2006/07, would last until the beginning of August. The start of the league in Ghana often differs each season. In the meantime, we mainly played tournaments and practice matches. Kotoko also had to compete in the CAF Champions League, but I wasn't registered for that.

At that time, I was already busy with my school, and it became increasingly difficult to combine this with football. After all, I was in Kumasi, and my school was in Accra. I got to a point where I had to make a choice. I decided then, in the spring of 2006, that it had been a good run. In the end, my last game was a friendly against Feyenoord Academy in Kumasi. I enjoyed my last game, even though it was just a friendly. When I realised my career was over, it went pretty smoothly. I still felt young at only 31 years old. I didn't think about it too much because I had my businesses to worry about.

So the end of my football career saw me go straight into taking care of my school. I was glad that I had something to occupy myself with, because it felt strange not to be a footballer all of a sudden. At that time, I didn't really have the energy or desire to look back on my career. Not even on everything that had happened outside of football, and my childhood. I didn't take the time for it. Nowadays I think a lot about everything that happened. Thinking about all those things like I do now wasn't possible then. I didn't want to deal with it. That's why I was busy with my school every day.

I had played my last game in the Asante Kotoko shirt. Online it says everywhere that I also played football for Jomo

Cosmos in South Africa, but that's a misunderstanding. In the spring of 2007 I finally started talking to Jomo Cosmos. That was only because I knew the owner, Jomo Sono, from my time in the Ghana national team when we played in the Africa Cup of Nations in South Africa in 1996. I met him there. Sono played with Pelé at New York Cosmos in 1977. In 1982 he bought a club in South Africa and renamed it after himself and after his old club, hence the name Jomo Cosmos.

Jomo wanted me to play football for Cosmos. He heard that I'd already ended my career but wanted me to play for him, although the club couldn't pay me. I didn't ask for a high salary at all, but they couldn't give me that amount either. I'd already started training at the club but in the end the negotiations came to nothing. After one or two weeks there it was clear that it wasn't going to become anything. I then went back to Ghana and didn't play a single game in South Africa. So I just trained, and nothing more.

I knew then that there was definitely no continuation of my football career, but I wasn't disappointed. I'd already said goodbye to Kotoko as a player. And at that time I was so busy with my school because I'd invested a lot of money in it. Not only had things gone wrong with a company of mine before, but other players I knew had also had problems setting up businesses in Ghana. I wanted to avoid that. That's why I focused on the school, and no longer on a career in football. That was definitely done.

Chapter 17

The football academy

WHEN MY career ended, I continued to follow football. I'm just a fan. I mainly looked forward and not back, but of course there were moments when I sometimes thought about my career, how things turned out, and how they could have gone differently. I kept facing it. When Ghana qualified for a World Cup for the first time, back in 2006, I thought back to 1994.

That was the year in which we should actually have qualified but we screwed it up. Of course I was happy that Ghana had managed to reach the finals, but at the same time that missed opportunity of the World Cup in 1994 came to the fore again. At the 2006 tournament I was only 31 years old. Would I have had a chance to play at that World Cup? How different could things have turned out in my career if I hadn't met Antonio Caliendo and my knee wasn't bothering me?

Just after finishing my career, our fifth child, Moesha, was born in May 2006. When Gloria became pregnant with Moesha I was happy, but also surprised, because I really didn't want any more children. After the death of Lisa in Germany and Diego in Argentina, I no longer dared to give it another try. I didn't want to go through what I went through with them again. In addition, all the children, with the exception of Latifah, had been delivered by Caesarean section. I didn't want to risk Gloria's health either. Eventually Moesha also had to be delivered by Caesarean section, but luckily she was born healthy. That was quite a relief.

Around 18 months after the 2006 World Cup, I was approached by the Ghanaian channel TV3. They asked if I wanted to work for them as a football analyst. That was before the Africa Cup of Nations in January 2008. They came to me because of my football experience, but also because I had a lot to say. After that they kept calling me for all kinds of international matches for Ghana, and also for the under-17 and under-20 teams, especially because I'd caused a furore with those teams in the past. I still do that along with other analysts, often former players, such as Sammy Kuffour. I don't do Ghanaian Premier League matches. I just can't combine that with my work at my football academy. I get paid for the TV work, and at the big tournaments I also get a contract for, for example, a month. In August 2016 I was even an analyst on South African television, at Kwasse TV. I am still regularly invited by them but unfortunately I often have to decline due to lack of time.

So after setting up my school in 2004 and having to deal with all the difficult regulations later on, I cancelled my earlier plans for a university. But I'd already bought a piece of land for that and in 2009 I started a cattle farm there. A good friend of mine was already in that business and said it would be a good investment. There were only minor risks involved. Before that I'd never thought about having a farm. That idea wasn't discussed until much later. It's crazy how things can play out sometimes. I partly financed the setting up of the farm by selling my house in Kumasi that I had built for my father, in 2008, when my half-brothers had all left too.

I started the farm with ten cows and one bull. After that I regularly bought a few more cows. I stopped when I had about 100 of them. Now I don't have to buy them anymore because enough calves are born. I only sell. The farm is quite simple, with one building where the employees eat and sleep. That's about all. Stables aren't necessary due to the warm weather in Ghana. All the challenges that came with my school were incomparable to setting up my farm, by the way. I had no such problems at all with the farm. The only risk is that suddenly cattle go missing, or that someone is trying to steal them. But if you have someone you trust and who arranges security well, it's perfectly manageable. And luckily that hardly happens. A large part of my land is fenced off, so that the cows cannot just run away at night. The animals also have no stamp or tag; the people who work with the animals just know which animals belong to them. If one escapes and is found, they can see for themselves if it's mine. The fact that the animals don't have a stamp or tag is also useful in the event that my cattle accidentally end up in another farmer's yard, where the animals eat something from the crops there. Without a tag, those farmers don't know that it's one of my cows!

The farm is a pretty easy way for me to make money in the short term. You can easily sell cows as there's always a demand for them. With the school it's of course very different. So, the investment in setting up the farm was well worth it. There are now about 500 head of cattle: mostly cows, but also about 150 goats and sheep. I sell quite a lot of livestock, particularly around Christmas and Ramadan. I especially sell goats a lot. The milk from the animals is sold by the farmers I hire, by the way. They can keep that money, in addition to their salary.

In February 2009 I was offered a job in football, out of nowhere. It was a trainer position at Sekondi Eleven Wise, a club that played in the Ghanaian Premier League at the time. I'd thought about a job as a coach because football remains my passion. But I wanted to focus on my school first and was in no rush. But in early 2009 the opportunity came suddenly, and it felt right. The management of Eleven Wise had approached me and it seemed like something interesting to me, but I had no coaching experience yet. I thought it would be a good idea to do that with someone else and I approached Charles 'CK' Akonnor, my former team-mate from the national team. He was about to leave for Germany because he wanted to become a coach there. He was even naturalised as a German; he had played football there for years. Because he had that ambition, I told him about the offer I'd been given and asked whether he was interested in it. He was. We then decided to work together at Eleven Wise. Charles would start as head coach and I would become an assistant. Charles already had that ambition to become head coach. The club's board also agreed.

At the beginning of 2009 we started at Eleven Wise. The 2008/09 season was then halfway through and was halted for a few weeks due to the Africa Cup of Nations. When the competition resumed, we immediately faced a difficult task. It was an away game against my last club, Asante Kotoko. However, we managed to win 2-1 just before the end. That was a good start for us. I ended up being an assistant coach for almost one year, until the end of 2009. The first season was pretty good and we finished eighth. However, the second season did not start well and we only got four points in the first six games. It wasn't much better halfway through the competition and the club wanted Charles to leave as head coach. He didn't have to go entirely, but he would instead become director of sports, and his successor was a German, Hans-Dieter Schmidt. I could have remained there as an assistant coach but it also seemed like a good time to stop. That job had given me the inspiration to start a football academy myself.

I had become very enthusiastic about that idea and soon after that I started getting it set up. I already had the passion and love for football. And to be involved with football: I preferred that much more than my school and farm. Nothing to the detriment of those, of course, but football has been in me from an early age. Later in 2017, Eleven Wise approached me again. This time they asked if I was interested in becoming CEO of the club. It was a nice offer, but I could never have combined that with my own football academy. The club is in another city and that would have been impossible given the time it would have taken me. I declined that offer, but I'm still in regular contact with them.

After making the decision about the football academy, I started looking for a good place to set it up. I visited several places but finally I started in Abreshia-Elmina, a small village. It's located near Elmina, a fishing village on the coast of Ghana. It's where the Portuguese established the first European settlement of West Africa in the 15th century. In Abreshia I was able to rent a plot of land with an empty building. I paid for that by selling my house in Kumasi, among other things. The start was with a simple accommodation and one football field. In August 2010 I 'officially' started my football academy. I called it the Glow Lamp Soccer Academy, the same name as my school. At first was very difficult. When they heard that I had set up a football academy, 300 boys came. There had to be two teams, divided into under-17s and under-19s. About 35 guys, that's all. That was a very difficult job, but in the end it worked.

I had to rent the land I was using for at least 15 years. But after a few years I bought 20 hectares of land a little further, about ten minutes' walk away. I in turn rent out the house with the land that I now must rent for a few more years to other people. Finally, in 2013, I slowly started building the facilities as they are at my new location. It was only from 2015 that we were able to make optimal use of it. People often don't know that my football school is located there. It is thought that I set this up, but that's not true. And that I now have three football fields and all these facilities: changing rooms, a few houses for the technical staff and players, and even a residence for entire teams that they can rent. Just in case they want to set up a training camp at my academy. It is a conscious choice. For the time being I choose to run my academy in relative peace. So far, it's going well. I started in 2010 with two teams and in 2018 I added an under-15 team.

It's not easy running the academy, although I do enjoy it a lot. When you start such an academy you also have to make sure that you do it well. But is it easy? No, definitely not. Only players who really want to make it come here, players in whom I see potential. If someone comes here to play football for fun, he is wasting his time, and mine too. Neither of us benefit from such a situation. It is in any case not common to play football at a club in Ghana as a hobby. Doing that in addition to your job, for example, is rare.

Football is just kind of an industry here. People do play football for fun in Ghana, but that happens on squares, open fields and riverbeds. Not at clubs.

Initially, at my academy we try to train players. But we also try to teach them to deal with other things that come with a possible career. Think of the whole Antonio Caliendo thing during my own career. I often use that example now. That's why I try to warn the players at my academy, so that they won't make the same mistakes I did. We tell them that you shouldn't just go into business with the first person who calls himself a football agent. When players are done learning here, we help them to choose a good agent. Success, or just the chance of success, attracts so-called agents who only want to make money off them. Ghanaian footballers end up all over the world because of this. Some guys are easy to persuade because they're eager. It doesn't take much to convince them and their parents to work with a certain agent. If such an individual tells you that he will ensure that you get a job somewhere and start earning money, most people will quickly give in. It's a difficult situation.

It is difficult to distinguish the good from the bad brokers. And at a young age you're already naive anyway. If you play at a club in Ghana and not abroad, you will soon hear that you're probably not good enough either, and that otherwise you have to go abroad as soon as possible, preferably to Europe, to earn money. Precisely because football is now seen as a revenue model in Ghana, the pressure from family is already great at an early age. As a result there's a chance that a player will do business with the first person who calls himself an agent that one encounters, and that is often not the best choice. But even then you still have to read and understand what you are signing for.

Fortunately, nowadays it's much easier to find out whether someone can be trusted and what that person has done in the past, or with whom he has worked. That makes a big difference. In that respect it's become a lot easier for the youngsters of today than when I was young. If I had today's technology back then, I'd only have to type in the name 'Antonio Caliendo' to find out everything about him. For example, it wasn't until years later that I learned that Caliendo had been given a ten-month suspended prison sentence in 1991 for tax evasion. And in 1992 he was arrested again because of an investigation into the finances of Hellas Verona in Italy. And I didn't know anything about this, while he was my agent at the time.

In addition to the business aspect, we also focus on the importance of education. I thank God every day for giving me my football career. But how different would it have been if I'd gone to school every day before? Then I could have gotten more out of my career. I use myself as an example to show what can happen if one doesn't receive a good education. Players really don't all have to go to college, as long as they get the basics. Make sure you can read and write well, make sure you know what your signature means, make sure you know what's in documents you sign. I mainly teach them the things that keep them from being cheated, as I have been cheated. Use the teachings throughout your football career and, when you're done, there's still plenty of time to learn other things. Although I know very well that it is sometimes very difficult to combine school and football.

If someone thinks they can make it in football, they should act as soon as possible. If such a player comes to my academy he has three to six months to prove himself. If I see enough potential, I will tell them. In that case he may stay longer. Players stay here for about three to four consecutive months. Then they have three or four weeks off. During this period, they often return to their families. It's the way the universities work here too. The guys who don't make it don't come back after that period. In their place come new guys who try. In the end players stay here for one year, sometimes two years, during which we try to help them succeed as footballers. The boys in whom we see a future as players will therefore stay here longer.

It is of course not realistic to think that everyone who walks around here will also become a professional. Only a few boys will actually do so. That's why I want to be clear as soon as possible to the boys and their parents at my academy – not only for ourselves, but also for them. Only a few of them will be good enough to become professional footballers, and few of them will leave for Europe. It's painful for those guys to invest their time in something that won't make them money. Then they would be better going to school or work. Incidentally, the boys at my academy also work in addition to playing football, or they still go to school.

We don't have scouts walking around, that's not how it works here. There are also no amateur clubs where you can scout. Interested parties call me or email me. After the procedure is made clear to them, they come by for about ten days. In it, about three matches are played in addition to several training sessions. If you're good, we'll see. It's that simple. When the players are 18 they're done here. I try to set them up at a club, but sometimes Ghanaian clubs also knock on the door themselves. Then they ask if I have a striker or goalkeeper who is suitable for them. Footballers from my academy play in the Ghanaian Premier League, and I also have players in Qatar. But you shouldn't be in Ghana for the big money. The clubs are struggling to find sponsors, with the result that there is little money available. As a result some clubs occasionally struggle to pay players at the end of the month. That's just sad. That is why they leave for any country where they can earn money and get paid. That is partly the reason why there are Ghanaian football players all over the world. Ghana is bursting with football talent.

* * *

Yaw Preko: 'What Nii says is correct. There's hardly any money coming in, mainly due to a lack of sponsors. It's difficult in Ghana to connect companies to you as a club. They have few opportunities to earn their money back. And no money also means low wages for the players. That's why they want to leave the country as soon as possible. But they leave way too fast. They go to Tanzania, to Zambia. Even there you can earn more than in Ghana. In this way, players for the clubs can hardly be kept here. So many new players have to be trained every year, because players leave quickly. They know that a footballer's career is relatively short, so they don't take time to build their career slowly. How long is the average career of a football player, ten years? If players go to Sudan, Tanzania or Zambia, it's because they can play football there for two or three years to earn a little money. If they stay in Ghana, they earn less. If they even get paid at all. So, the choice is easy then. If you as a footballer are lucky enough to get a job elsewhere, then you go.'

Nii: 'Freddy Adu is also from Ghana, although he played football for the United States national team. He was once called "the new Pelé" at a young age, but he too could not live up to that. He once said in an interview that players in Ghana "just disappear". Not literally, but I know what he means. Ghanaian players simply have to earn money, also for their families in Ghana. So, they go wherever they can make money. Even if they have to play football in a distant country, in a lower division or at an unknown club. Talented players sometimes choose this too quickly and, in this way, they kill their own career. One minute they are known, but then they choose a certain country or a certain club and then you never hear from them again. So that's what Adu means. That's not only in Ghana, but it also applies to other African countries. But the background is of course also different. Footballers from poorer countries simply play football to earn money.'

* * *

Nowadays many boys want to come here to play football. It's become big business. Pleasure is no longer a priority. That started in the years after we became world champions with Ghana under-16s in 1991. After people realised that there's a lot of money to be made in football, the mentality changed. Within a few years players from Ghana's youth teams and the national team almost all played abroad. The generation after me went to the World Cup three times in a row since 2006. Everyone got to know those great footballers, everyone knows what they earn. Parents began to encourage their children to play as well. In my youth it was completely different, the opposite in fact. Children were not allowed to play football because they had to work or help with the household. When I was little and playing football, I was beaten and abused at home for playing football. And now? Now children are urged by their parents to play football. Times have changed.

While I was setting up my football academy in 2010, my mother passed away. I had a better relationship with her than with my father, but it wasn't the real mother-son relationship like back in the day either, even though my mother was very sweet. I left her house when I was 10 or 11 years old, and for the next few years I had little contact with her. Only when I played football at Anderlecht did the contact improve again and we developed a good relationship. That's also the reason that I bought a house for her at that time. In later years we talked a lot about the past; what happened and what we missed. My mother later told me that I was destined to be a football player. I was born backwards. Not with my head first, but with my feet.

The death of my mother had a nasty aftermath. I decided to sell the house where she lived. I had bought that house for her in 1993, and the papers were also in my name. But after her death I couldn't find those papers. It turned out that Odartie had them in his possession. He thought the house belonged to the whole family. I explained to him that it was my house because I had bought it, but he didn't want to hear it. He even took me to court because he thought it was a family house and that he was allowed to live there. But it quickly became apparent that the house was mine, so I won that case. I thought it was very ungrateful of him because I'd also helped him out in England. Since then, things have never worked out between us.

About six months later that year I was again startled by an obituary. My other brother Odarquaye passed away unexpectedly. It turned out that, like my father, he drank a lot. His liver also stopped working. I didn't know about that at all; I had no idea he drank that much. But there were other things I didn't know about him. After his death it turned out that he had six children! I didn't know that at all. It was bizarre. I still support a few of them financially now and then.

* * *

Oliver König: 'In 2011, Nii and I crossed paths again. I was active in Ghana myself, and at the time had invested in a football academy in Kumasi. In return I would receive ten per cent of the transfer fee in the event of a transfer. At one point Frank Acheampong was sold from that academy to Anderlecht. The fee was transferred to the account of my partner, who fled immediately after transferring that money. I never saw any of that money. For eight months he seemed to have disappeared from the face of the earth, until he suddenly came back with the announcement that the money was gone. I'd already withdrawn from that project at that point.

'Around that time, I heard that Nii had also started a football academy. We started talking about a renewed collaboration. I would invest in his academy and in return I would get a percentage of every transfer. We did that for several years, but eventually our collaboration ended in the autumn of 2015. We had a disagreement about running the football academy and we couldn't figure it out. Nii then started to focus on his academy on his own and I got into another project.'

Nii: 'The collaboration has ended due to a difference of opinion about the course to be followed by the football academy: about the finances, about the transfers of players. If you aren't in agreement, you must stop. Oliver wanted to do things differently because he had invested, but some things I didn't want to change. Then it just ends there. The collaboration wasn't stopped in any strange way. We just put an end to it.'

Chapter 18

Deceit

THERE ARE several things that football players sometimes face that remain hidden from the public. You have to deal with many issues: problems at home, problems with football, problems with family. The pressure on many African footballers is enormous. You can easily succumb to it in the end. On average, the career of an African player is not as long as that of one from Europe. And everything I went through when I was young – I didn't know about anything then, neither professionally nor emotionally. That's why I didn't know I was married to a bad woman. I find it difficult to talk about this stuff.

In the years after the end of my career, I was mainly concerned with my school. It was getting bigger every year. By the end of 2009 the number of students had reached 400, about the maximum that we could handle. That was very satisfying. In 2009 I became assistant coach of Sekondi

Eleven Wise, so from that moment on I could no longer deal with the school on a daily basis. After my period at Eleven Wise my time was mainly spent setting up my football academy. Everything was actually going well at that point. I felt happy and was doing what I wanted to do. I couldn't complain.

But in the meantime, something bad had been building up. Something terrible that I never thought possible. I hope no one ever has to go through this. In this book I deliberately did not pay too much attention to my relationship with Gloria and the children. Yes, Gloria has been a big part of my career, so my relationship with her does come into play. But I made a point of keeping rather quiet about that relationship, and that's for a reason.

Gloria and the kids were always with me, no matter what club I played at, except at Shandong Luneng in China. Latifah and Khadija were taught at international schools abroad when they got older. I raised them and lovingly cared for them. I remember that Latifah was born in Ghana, while I was in England at the time. When I first saw her, wow. Her skin was very dark, very black, just like mine. I had no reason to suspect anything strange.

By 2013 Latifah was old enough to study. Gloria wanted her to study in England. But schooling over there cost $26,000 per year! I didn't have that kind of money at all. I had put a lot of money into the farm, the school and my football academy. Besides, if Latifah were to leave for England, we couldn't afford not to let Khadija, who was just a little younger, go in the same direction later on. And maybe we wouldn't have been able to afford for Moesha to do it a few years later either. So just calculate what that would cost us. I told Gloria that too. We couldn't let Latifah start this studying knowing she wouldn't be able to finish it, so she just had to go to a university in Ghana. They are also fine, by the way. If I could earn a little more money in the future, she might be able to do her master's in England. That was only one year. But Gloria didn't want that and we disagreed about it. She walked away angrily, and not much later she came back. Out of nowhere she suddenly said she wanted a divorce.

Normally this wouldn't be a reason to divorce. I didn't understand. It was very strange. I felt a mixture of all kinds of emotions. It wasn't fun, and naturally I was surprised and sad. On the other hand, for me it was an immediate confirmation of what people had sometimes tried to make clear to me: that she did everything for the money. I was very sad, but somehow it also felt like a relief. Later that day Gloria appeared in the doorway of the room where I was sitting. She asked what she would get from the divorce. I then said, 'If you want to go, go ahead.' I was done with her. I said if she wanted to go through with the divorce, she should get her lawyer involved. From the way she reacted I could tell she didn't mind the divorce at all.

It quickly became clear to me that there was more to it than our quarrel over Latifah's study. Money apparently also played a role, but there were also rumours about infidelity. Certain things then fell into place. Just before that fight with Gloria I'd already heard a rumour about Elikem Kumordzie, someone who participated in *Big Brother Africa*. He had mentioned one of my children on TV by name. I was angry because he interfered with my children. Then I went to investigate and received reports from several quarters that he had been cheating with Gloria. I confronted her about it, but she said it wasn't true. I had no hard evidence and she denied everything. What was I to do then? She filed for divorce not long after, so I knew more then.

Not much later I also hired a lawyer. That was also the day I left our house. Gloria stayed there. The divorce itself was never the problem; that was actually settled fairly quickly. But Gloria immediately started talking about what she would be left with from the divorce. She didn't want to leave our house until we had agreed on something. I said we would do that through our lawyers. Because nothing had been agreed yet, she didn't want to leave, probably afraid of getting nothing. So I just left. I took some of my stuff from the house and left for a hotel.

Gloria really turned it into a lawsuit. That wasn't necessary for me at all; I thought we would work it out. But then she came with her demand. She claimed half of all my possessions. Also half the value of my school, the football academy, the farm, houses. Everything, while she was the one who probably had cheated. During that time, I also heard other rumours, that the suspected affair with Kumordzie had not been an isolated instance and that Gloria had cheated with other men as well. I even heard rumours that my children weren't mine. The problem, however, was that I had no proof of Gloria's cheating. We had to collect that, because then we would stand a lot stronger during the trial.

The first time I was in court didn't feel right. I had never been to a court of law. Gloria was the first to tell her story and answer all kinds of questions, then it was my turn. The first judge to intervene in the lawsuit immediately ruled in favour of Gloria to be allowed to stay in my house. The house I had built, with my earned money. And do you know why? Gloria had falsely accused me of visiting her and the children with a jerry can of gas, suggesting that I wanted to burn them in the house. The judge then ruled that I posed a threat to Gloria and the children. He also gave me only an hour to collect some more personal items from the house. I was not allowed to take anything else with me.

However, I didn't take the opportunity to pick up some stuff. That was the advice of my lawyer. He didn't think I should give Gloria any reason to spread rumours. Suppose something happened to her at that very moment, or that she would do something to herself. All I had to do was get close to her and she could use that to say I'd done something to her. That wouldn't be the first time. Gloria was capable of anything, as evidenced by the accusation that I wanted to set the house on fire. But also, during our marriage it happened a few times that she falsely accused me. That was for domestic violence. I would have said something she didn't like. She then would go to the DOVVSU, the Domestic Violence & Victim Support Unit, and accuse me of violence. The first time they believed her, and I was arrested. Then I even spent a few hours behind bars before I could make them see that what she said was wrong. Later she did that a few more times.

Even that agency warned me about her at one point. They told me she was telling them things that couldn't be true. Why? No idea. Sometimes she would go out and come home very late at night, and I would ask why she was back so late. She didn't like that and then she would make those kinds of accusations. The first time was after we had been together for a few years. She was supposed to go out for a drink, but didn't come home until 2am. Then don't expect me to applaud her. One time she even went so far as to cut herself, after which she accused me at those authorities of doing that. Bizarre.

So for the trial we needed evidence about Gloria's cheating and the fact that she had lied to me outright. It was mainly to show that she was not entitled to what she demanded, namely half of all my possessions. I decided to talk to some of her friends. But without their knowledge, I secretly recorded those conversations. Maybe they'd say something about Gloria that I could use, even if it was just something small. And then, out of nowhere, one of her friends suddenly called out the names of Latifah's and Khadija's fathers. In other words, I was not their father.

I didn't want to believe it; I couldn't believe it. I kept trying to stay calm in that moment. I did not know the men mentioned personally but knew who one of them was. That was an ex of Gloria, the man she was with before she met me. I asked that friend why she never told me earlier, but she was afraid I would confront Gloria. So she kept her mouth shut to me.

In court, Gloria denied everything, as always. But there was still no hard evidence, just rumours about the paternity of Latifah and Khadija. But not long after, someone else contacted me. That was a well-known former boxer, Ike Quartey, who between 1994 and 1998 was the WBA world welterweight champion. A friend of Quartey's was friends with a friend of Gloria's and had heard something too. He came to me and told me that my youngest child, Moesha, probably also had a different father, that I wasn't her biological father either. I confronted Gloria about that too but she just said Quartey was crazy.

I don't know what Gloria was doing when I wasn't there. At the time of all those rumours, I started thinking back to certain moments in the past. Could I have suspected something? That made me start to doubt everything. After Lisa passed away, I said I didn't want any more children. I didn't want to risk going through that pain again that I had already felt twice with Diego and Lisa. I would have loved to have another son, but I didn't want to take that risk anymore. When Gloria got pregnant again, I was surprised. Friends of hers already knew it wasn't my child, but they didn't start talking until years later. That was at the time of the trial. That has never happened before. But Gloria told me at that moment that she wanted another son for me. That was her excuse. I would have loved to have a son and would never have kept it a secret. She used that as an excuse.

I also remembered my 1991 youth World Cup gold medal. In July 2013, shortly before all the Gloria stuff started, it was stolen from my house. I was at my football academy at the time. When I came back, my gold medal was gone. Other medals I had won were still there. Only the gold was missing. It must have been stolen by someone who came to our house; friends of Gloria, or Gloria herself. That medal has a lot of sentimental value to me. But it was also worth a lot of money and could be sold for a lot of money. I reported the theft but I never found out who stole it. Gloria must have had something to do with it, I'm 100 per cent sure. But I can't prove it.

Gloria's girlfriend, who claimed that I was not the father of Latifah and Khadija, advised me during a conversation to do a DNA test. I had never heard of that. I showed my lawyer that conversation and he then told me what it was and where we could do it. In the end, along with a doctor, I went to the schools of the children. The doctor needed a DNA sample from them. I came up with a ruse with that doctor. I would tell the kids I had an infection in my throat and the doctor would therefore also want to examine the children, because they could supposedly also have that infection. If they didn't do something about it, they might lose their voices too. Latifah and Khadija then agreed to swab some cheek mucus with a cotton swab. They opened their mouths, and the doctor was able to take a sample from their mouths. Then I went to Moesha's school to do the same. When we were done the doctor said it would take me two weeks to get the results, but it ended up taking a month.

One day the doctor called to say that I could come by for the results. I went to his office, we sat down and he asked how long I'd been with Gloria, and if they had been good years. I had first met her in 1993 when I played football for Anderlecht, and it was now 2013. So, I'd been with her for about 20 years. He didn't beat around the bush. He said, 'Nii, I'm sorry, but all three children are not yours.' I said, 'What?' He explained everything to me calmly. At that moment I was shaking all over and started to cry. I wanted to get out of there right away. I couldn't stay any longer. Then I immediately called my lawyer Kizito Beyuo and went to see him. He apologised and sympathised with me. He said it was very hard but also told me to control myself, and that I shouldn't do anything stupid. That warning was not for nothing.

As I was driving back home in my car, I thought I'd better kill myself. My whole life had collapsed. Everything had turned out to be a lie and I had been greatly embarrassed. I decided at that point to put an end to it. At home I had a gun, which I was allowed to possess because I had a permit. But in the end I couldn't. Apparently, I still had the strength not to do it. I then gave the gun to someone else before deciding to use it after all. I'm really glad I didn't in the end. I'm glad I'm still alive.

The following days were extremely tough. In any case, I was glad I got through that time. I thanked God that I was still alive, and that I learned everything at that moment. I could still have children if I wanted to. My own biological children. I thought about that. What if I was 60 or 70 and only then found out? What would I have done then? So much went through my mind in those days. Despite everything that had happened with Gloria, I wasn't expecting that DNA test result. I never thought those kids wouldn't be mine. However, my lawyer wanted to be sure, because if those children turned out not to be mine we would of course have to use that against Gloria in the lawsuit.

It is very sad to look back now and see how much money I spent on the five children. And to the woman who betrayed me, who hurt me, who still has some of my possessions and who sued me. Money isn't the most important thing, of course, but I've spent a lot on them. I spent so much money on Diego and Lisa alone. And the other kids too. I gave them everything: a good education, private schools abroad. It's sad and painful.

After the results of that DNA test, I thought a lot about Diego and Lisa. I will never know if they were my biological children. I haven't done a DNA test with them, as I don't have ampoules of blood from them. I wouldn't know if you could dig them up to collect DNA material. Perhaps Diego's and Lisa's lives were doomed to fail; that they wanted to spare me the same grief. I started to think things like that. Afterwards I heard all kinds of rumours about Gloria, that she cheated even during her pregnancies. But even for this I must thank God. What if Diego and Lisa had survived and I found out after all these years that they wouldn't have been my biological children either? Then I would have suffered even more. And maybe Diego and Lisa too.

After letting it all sink in, we contacted the court to say that the children were not mine and that we had done a DNA test. Gloria knew all along that they weren't my kids, of course, so she couldn't help but admit it in the end. But then she came up with another excuse. She said she wanted to protect me because I was impotent. That's why she wouldn't have said that to me. But then she said I knew that too, and that I knew that that's why the children couldn't be mine. The reason I would be impotent is that during my football career I would have ingested things that would have led to that – injections and the like. But Gloria was lying again.

That *Big Brother* participant Elikem later admitted that he had an affair with Gloria. It turned out that he had been cheating with Gloria for four years. At first he denied it, but later he admitted everything. He has apologised to the media. Not to me, but only to the media, because he lied to them. The entire lawsuit, the verdicts and all the details have meanwhile been widely reported in the press. All of Ghana knew about it.

In the meantime, I continued to run my football academy as best I could. There I could relax and forget about all my problems, even if only for a moment. I had been staying in a hotel for a few months, during which time I met Ruweida. I had been working for various football programmes for a few years as a regular guest analyst. Ruweida was best known for Ghana's Most Beautiful Beauty Pageant 2008, in which she made it to the final. After that, she also acted in various films and presented TV shows. My football programmes happened to be in the same studio. I've known her for a while, since 2009 or 2010. When Gloria and I were separated for a while, she sent someone to ask for my phone number and I gave it. That's how we got in touch and not much later we started dating.

A lot went through my mind during that period. I thought about having a spiritual curse cast on Gloria: Antoa Nyamaa, a river god of the Ashanti. But that's a big thing, and a very bad thing. Speaking that curse to settle personal feuds is also risky for me, and would also cause me misery. Sometimes I still think about it, but it's really not necessary because I know Gloria will be punished anyway for the things she has done. Ruweida helped me a lot during that difficult period. She advised me not to do such crazy things. She also persuaded me to leave the hotel where I was staying and be with her. Then we first lived in her parents' house for about three months.

And then Ruweida got pregnant. With my baby. That was very good news in those difficult times. In May 2014 my first real daughter was born: Malaika. I can't describe how I felt; I was very emotional knowing Malaika was my first biological child. Logical, of course, after that whole affair involving Gloria and her children. It also came at a good time, because that way I could immediately prove that Gloria was lying. That I could show that I wasn't impotent at all, as she had claimed in the trial. With that I was also immediately liberated from the image that Gloria was trying to paint of me.

The moment Ruweida found out she was pregnant, we decided to rent a house. Gloria was still in my old house and I didn't want Ruweida to give birth in her parents' home. We just needed somewhere of our own. I then rented a place near my school, while Gloria lived in my house. That's what the judge had decided. I found that statement bizarre; it made no sense. My entire marriage to her, for 19 years, had been one big lie. Our children turned out not to be mine, she spent my money on herself and her children, and then she drags me to court? It does not make any sense.

We therefore conducted an investigation into that judge. And what turned out to be the case? He once went to the same school as Gloria. My lawyer then went to court and saw to it that he was removed from the case. We then got a different judge, but he also ruled the same. He may have been influenced by the first one; they often know each other. Of course we appealed, and fortunately that ruling was reversed. So, in practice I could now return to my house, but I've decided not to. In the meantime, there's a chance Gloria sold all kinds of my stuff. But stuff is, after all, just stuff. I think it's much more important that I'm still alive.

I've never thought too much about that old stuff of mine.

Meanwhile, the lawsuit has been going on for years. Why is everything taking so long? Only the Lord knows. I have no idea. Gloria has already changed lawyers five times. She keeps delaying the process. I'm the one who suffers, she's not. She's in no hurry. She's been in my house for years, with my belongings, while I've been renting a house for a long time. Sometimes she doesn't even show up to court, and always has excuses. The case is greatly delayed. I feel like I'm being punished twice.

In June 2017, the case finally seemed to be coming to an end. The final verdict was made, and it came out that she had to leave my house. She was still going to get two million cedi, about $360,000, and the old three-bedroom apartment my mom lived in. She would also get a car, a Toyota Verso. I actually thought that was way too much but I agreed because I wanted to be finished with it all. Gloria turned that down. She's greedy. She should be satisfied with that. She could start all over with that proposal, and yet she declined. I expected that she would be satisfied with that, because it was much more than she deserves. I was glad to finally be able to return to my home but Gloria appealed again. I now rent out the apartment she was assigned. As long as the appeal is pending, the judge allows her to stay in my house. Bizarre, especially because of the last statement.

There has been twice now a ruling saying she had to leave, and suddenly there's a judge who says she can stay there again until the case is settled. Very weird. Until the case reoccurs, we must therefore be patient. That's what we're waiting for now. But that day will come. I have steady contact with my lawyer Iris about the next steps because we want to keep the pressure on. Iris works in Kizito's office. I started with Kizito, but Iris mainly takes care of my business. And things can get crazy here. Sometimes a case can last five years, sometimes even ten years. But however the case ends, I have already been punished. I am innocent. I don't understand how she can do that to me. My 19-year marriage to Gloria was one big lie. I was lied to, she cheated on me and I took care of three children for years that weren't mine. And then she stretches the lawsuit for years, so that I don't live in my own house and have to rent a house for years. I am being punished when she should be punished. She should be locked up for everything she did to me. There's no reason to let her live in that house.

What sometimes happens in Ghana is that people are bribed. Maybe she's been doing that with those judges and is offering them money. No one is investigating that either.

That's bad stuff, it's beyond frustrating. I have no idea when this will end. There are plenty of people who take the law into their own hands because of things like this. Some people commend me for having reacted the way I did. I didn't do anything crazy in the end; I behaved. But there are plenty of other examples of people who can't muster the patience. They kill their husbands or wives, go to jail or commit suicide. I can imagine why people might do the wrong thing.

After I heard that my children weren't mine and after all the provocations from my ex-wife, I also thought about suicide. I almost did it. But I'm glad I didn't. I am lucky enough to have been patient and met Ruweida. You want justice, that's why there are lawsuits. But look where I am now. What did I do to deserve that? It's sad. But I lay fate in the Lord's hands.

Chapter 19

The future

BY NOW I also have a second daughter, Manal Manha Lamptey. She was born in August 2016. And on 13 November 2019 my son Mahal Nii Lamptey Jr. was born. I am now very happy with my two daughters and my son and with Ruweida. It's very nice to be with her. She is warm and friendly, and she works hard. That was different with Gloria. Ruweida cares about people and is a warm person. But she can also be very fierce. And she has studied. I also set up a shop with her so that she can sell and do her own things, a beauty salon, with pedicure and hairdressing and lots more. And now she also works a lot in the school, because I spend a lot of time at my football academy, a few hours away. I'm very grateful to Ruweida and her family, who have helped me a lot.

A few months before Manal's birth, I received some shocking news that Stephen Keshi had passed away unexpectedly. I was very sad, which makes sense. I can never repay what Stephen did for me. Not only did he take me to Europe, but he also took care of me during those first months. He gave me shelter and food and advised me on everything. When I heard the news of his passing, I felt like I had lost a father. Stephen died of a heart attack, which some people believe was the result of his wife's death. She had died of cancer seven months earlier and Stephen sometimes seemed to have difficulty coping with her death. Stephen was a legend during his career, but later also as a coach. Under his leadership Togo qualified for the World Cup for the first time in 2006. And in 2013, as Nigeria's national team manager, he won the Africa Cup of Nations and they qualified for the 2014 World Cup. I won't soon forget him, that's for sure.

Alhaji Salifu Abubakar passed away in August 2017 after a short illness. I have of course experienced a lot with Salifu. He died a prosperous man, thanks in part to me. After I signed my first contract with Anderlecht, I had him come to Belgium because I felt I owed him that after he had done so much for me. Cornerstones received a transfer fee from Anderlecht, after which Salifu in turn also received an amount from them. But he thought that was too little and he was entitled to more. I transferred a portion of my first pay cheque, I believe it was $13,000, to him. He invested that money and at one point had several houses in Ghana. A few years later we had a disagreement when I married Gloria, and at the end of my career he was on the board of Asante Kotoko when I signed with that club. I went to his funeral and offered my condolences to his family. Sometimes I still have contact with his relatives and, when I have time and I'm in the area, I go and have a look at Kaloum Stars.

Despite those kinds of sad moments, everything continues, and of course, football too. At the moment football in Ghana is under a lot of pressure, partly due to a major corruption scandal. Several referees and officials have already been suspended as a result of the investigation, including the former president of the Ghana Football Association, Kwesi Nyantakyi. One of the journalists who investigated all the abuses, Ahmed Husein, was even shot. In addition, there's little money involved in football here. As a result, the second teams, which used to be at every club, have almost disappeared. There are only a few clubs that work with a second team. But that'll also work out. Football is currently in a slump, but it'll recover. Fortunately, my academy is doing well. In 2018 I started with a third team, the under-15s team. The future also looks good in that regard.

As for my relationship with Gloria, over the years I had never doubted it, even when it was going a little less smoothly. There were, of course, those moments. But I never thought to end the relationship. The image of Gloria as a gold-digger is correct in hindsight, but during our time together I had no problem with it. I gave her things. And I was young, I had little to compare it with regarding how it should be otherwise. In the end I must conclude that she contributed to the fact that my career didn't go well at a later stage. Unfortunately, some things you only realise afterwards.

A few years ago, when I found out about my ex-wife's cheating, I also started to really think about my career and my childhood. The football, the pain, the things I'd been through; it really got me thinking. Could I have prevented anything? Should I have done things differently? Sometimes I sit alone in my bedroom. Then I cry. Then I feel the pain of the past, and I feel very sad. I then put on a movie as a distraction, but then if it's one where something sad happens, then I imagine I'm that person. I put myself completely into what's happening in the film. I then get very emotional and the tears flow down my cheeks. Of course, I'm sometimes sad about everything I went through in my youth and during my football career, but that case with my ex-wife and the children was really the low point in my life. I hope no man has to go through such a thing. That was a very bad experience.

I no longer speak to the children I raised. I've found out the names of the real fathers of Latifah and Moesha, but I do not know them directly. Khadija's father is Gloria's ex-boyfriend, the man she was with before I started dating her. The last time I saw them as my own children, as their father, was when I was with them when we did that DNA test. That was also the last time I spoke to them. They were living with Gloria, while I had already left the house some time earlier. After the results of that test, I was of course shocked. Once the truth set in I started to look at the children differently. In the years that followed, I also decided that it was better not to have any contact with them. I didn't want any information to get to Gloria through them.

The lawsuit is still ongoing. But the children are victims as well. They are of course under the influence of their mother, so I have no idea what they think about me now. But I have nothing against them. Latifah tried to contact me some time ago but for now I am unable to do so. I have no problem with it, but at least I want to wait until the lawsuit is settled. If there is contact again afterwards, I don't mind at all.

The challenges I faced as a child, as crazy as it may sound, have made me the strong man I am today. If I hadn't experienced all those things in my youth and in my career, I would have missed a certain hardness. Then I would have committed suicide long ago. But I hope other kids don't go through the same thing I used to. It was so hard, so very hard, so mean sometimes. I still thank God every day that I have overcome all this.

I don't know what the future will bring. Despite the continuing lawsuit, I am confident of a good outcome no matter how long it takes. But I don't really care about that case anymore. It has become a formality for me. I am engaged to Ruweida, so marrying her is also in the planning. Everything else is going as it should with my school and my football academy. Everyone knows the school; we deliver a lot of good students. At the time, it was almost the only private school. Today there are numerous private schools. Perhaps because mine was successful; you are then often imitated. But I don't worry about that because education is still the best gift you can give your child. That is why it's good that other people are now investing money in it.

I'm slowly expanding my football academy, and the accommodation is also getting better bit by bit. In Ghana, the talent keeps coming. Hopefully that continues, because almost all the places where I used to play football are fully built up. As a result, the colts clubs have had an increasingly difficult time in recent years, while those are where children learn to play football. In the near future I'd like to establish a partnership with a European club. Anderlecht or PSV would of course be my preference, with the aim of sending a player on trial at that club once in a while.

My farm is also doing well, although I'm not too involved with it. I've appointed someone there, someone I trust. He in turn has recruited several employees who now run the farm. When I go there, I speak to the boss I have appointed and do all business with him. Because during the week I'm mainly present at my football academy, I'm no longer busy with my school on a daily basis. Every Monday I have an appointment with the school principal and an accountant to make sure everything is going well. In addition, I am of course still responsible for everything that happens. And every month I also have to arrange the salary of all employees, so that everyone gets their pay on time. I'm not there often, but Ruweida is, and she takes care of the day-to-day business. And I trust the people who work there. But it isn't easy, especially everything related to social insurance and taxes and the like.

I am very grateful for what I've achieved in football. The highlight is that I became world champion with Ghana under-16s. I still have the trophies I got for being named man of the match during that tournament. I later gave one to my mother, one is in my house on the grounds of my football academy, one is in the office at my school, and one is in my house where Gloria still lives. I also won the under-20 Africa Championship and a silver medal at the under-20 World Cup, I played football for the Ghanaian national team, I attended three Africa Cup of Nations tournaments (with one silver medal) and I have a unique bronze medal won at the Olympics. I played football at big clubs like PSV, Aston Villa and Anderlecht, where I became a champion of Belgium twice. And with Asante Kotoko I also became a champion. I have everything a footballer should get in his career. And no, I didn't end up with huge buckets of money. But I am very proud. And I'm very happy with the money I've earned, and to be able to give something back to society here. Look at my school, look at my football academy.

I cannot say that my football career has left me with many friends with whom I am still in contact. I've been in touch with Ron Atkinson, my manager at Aston Villa and Coventry City for a while. But that didn't last long. Same story with Dwight Yorke. I still have occasional contact with Kalusha Bwalya, with whom I played at PSV, also because of the position he held as an official at the African Football Association, the CAF. But I have to say I've never been good at keeping in touch. Apparently, I'm not the person who puts a lot of effort into that. I still have a lot of contact with other Ghanaian former players, especially with the generation of players from 1991 to 1993. If there is something wrong with one of them, we all try to help him.

Fortunately, the people in Ghana respect me. They still know my name and career, and what I have meant to Ghana. The name and fame are still there. When I went abroad as a youngster, there were a few other players from Ghana who were already overseas, such as Tony Yeboah and Abédi Pelé. I wasn't the first, but I was one of the first of my generation to leave. That eventually opened doors for other players. Some of them still thank me for that to this day, despite the stories that have appeared in the media about me because of that lawsuit. Luckily, for most people that's an afterthought. And that's very nice. I'm grateful for that. The respect is everywhere, whether it's football players, just anyone on the street or a police officer. At the time, I made the right choice to leave. It was scary at times, it was a dangerous decision, but ultimately the right one.

I will also always be reminded of the words of the great Pelé, who said I would become his successor. That never happened. Even now I often hear that one sentence in the media when people talk about me – that I would step into his shoes. And indeed, I haven't been able to live up to those expectations. If that comparison had never been made, many people would be speaking of me very differently now. The comparison was ultimately not fair. If it were true, I would have played at Barcelona, Real Madrid or Manchester United, the really big clubs. That never happened. But does that mean I failed as a footballer? Of course not. I am not a failure. I am a survivor. A survivor who refuses to be destroyed.